**On the Spot:**
Football as a Profession

To the memory of Charlie Roberts
and Billy Meredith, who helped
to pave the way

# On the Spot
## Football as a
## Profession

Derek Dougan and
Percy M. Young

Stanley Paul, London

Stanley Paul & Co Ltd
3 Fitzroy Square, London W1

An imprint of the Hutchinson Publishing Group

London Melbourne Sydney Auckland
Wellington Johannesburg Cape Town
and agencies throughout the world

First published 1974
© Derek Dougan and Percy M. Young 1974

Set in Monotype Baskerville
Printed in Great Britain by The Anchor Press Ltd
and bound by Wm. Brendon & Son Ltd
both of Tiptree, Essex

ISBN 0 09 121340 1

# Contents

# Introduction

We share a common passion for football, but have come to it from different backgrounds. For one of us football has been a profession and a means of livelihood; for the other it has been a meaningful experience within a different profession. Both of us have seen the game in the raw – in places remote from famous centres of football – but have come together in fraternal association in Wolverhampton.

The profession of football has always been, and remains, a hard one. But the football club and the individual player have important functions to perform within the community – whether in Workington or in Wolverhampton.

This book sets out to show the importance of the game. The game, however, only exists because of the player. It concerns us greatly that ever since football became professionalized the efforts of the player have rarely received adequate credit. This may at first seem hard to understand. This is one reason why this book needed to be written. But while we pay special attention to the player as an individual we are also concerned for the game as a whole.

In Britain, football is to be regarded as a way of life, with some kind of common purpose. We have examined the game – the one as a deeply involved professional of almost twenty years, the other as an historian – and set down what we have seen and experienced. We know the game as it was, but also as it is, and, perhaps, as it could be.

In this connection we look forward to the not far distant time when the professional footballer plays a more important part in administration and legislation.

We wrote this book before the Report of the Commission on Industrial Relations appeared in July 1974, but note that the Report complements most of our conclusions. Since the beginning, reports on this great institution of football have come out at regular intervals, the last being that of the CIR. Few industries have been so extensively examined, and so little done as a result. The only fundamental changes in the interests of the players, as our researches show, have come from the deliberations and actions of their own professional organization.

Although this is in every sense of the word a joint effort, we consider it imperative that our two styles are shown separately. The words of Derek Dougan, therefore, are set in italics. The illustrations are to be regarded as an essential part of the argument and they are listed in their appropriate places in the Index.

We are grateful to the Secretary and staff of the PFA for their unfailing helpfulness, especially in putting the invaluable records of the Association at our disposal.

D.D.
P.M.Y.

*August 1974*

# 1. Growing Up

*'I used to think that everything started at
three and finished at twenty to five . . .'*

*As far as the ordinary spectator is concerned, football belongs to ninety
minutes on a Saturday afternoon (in some European countries on Sunday
as well). He may fit in an extra session on* TV *in mid-week and – if
very keen – a half-hour of radio or* TV *round-up before the Saturday
match. But all he really thinks about – oblivious to everything else –
is that ninety minutes.*

*When, however, we begin to look at the subject in depth we see how
vast it really is. The development of football in the modern world,
indeed, is one of the most amazing examples of a 'growth industry'
ever known.*

As we now recognize it football is only a little more than a
hundred years old, for it gained independence only with the
setting up of the Football Association in London in 1863. Eight
years after this momentous event the FA Challenge Cup Competition was inaugurated. From that there is a direct line to
the 'World Cup', if only because from this first Cup came all
others.

The first step in this particular direction was the establishment in 1885 of a body called the International Football
Association Board. It is true that this contained only the governing bodies of football of England, Scotland, Ireland, and
Wales, but even that is remarkable in view of the short time
available for expansion up to that point. The year 1885 was
important in another way. For on 20 July the principle of
professionalism was accepted in England. (The other British
Associations came into line a little later.) Events moved fast.
Three years after the legalization of the professional, the Football League – with twelve founder clubs from the north and
the Midlands – was born.

Just after the turn of the century the rapid spread of the

game in foreign fields (due to the pioneer tours of British teams) pointed to the inadequacy of purely national associations in dealing with increasingly complex international matters. In 1904 an international organization – La Fédération Internationale de Football Association, better known as the FIFA– was inaugurated in Paris on a European basis. This took time to gather strength, but from the start it was clear that it was only an organization of this kind that could bring an over-all sense of control and unanimity into what by now was the most widespread and international of all games. The English Association, setting the trend for the other home bodies, with a misplaced sense of dignity that was sometimes to appear as an unfortunate characteristic, set itself apart.

At the same time, this detachment was not wholly dishonourable. The FA was concerned that the distinction between amateur and professional that had been agreed in 1885 should not be obscured by amateurs being in fact professionals. It has taken a hundred years to clear this finally, to the great advantage of everyone concerned. But the difficulties that appeared in the early days of football as a public institution developed alarmingly. The problem was made much more trying because of its international implications as football extended its hold across national frontiers.

In the international sphere the British amateurs won the football competition within the Olympics in 1908 and 1912. There were doubts as to whether all participants really upheld the true Olympic ideal as then understood. The more things change, the more they remain the same!

So it was that in the Polish national team that knocked England out of the 1974 World Cup there were most of the players who had gained the Olympic Games title two years earlier. It was, however, only the rather stuffy-minded British who noticed this as being remarkable. It may be pointed out, though, that the modern Olympics are still bedevilled by the same over-all problem to which the English football administrators of 1885, to their honour, found an answer.

A quick run-over of the first half-century of regularized football activity gives sufficient hard fact to suggest that the game was more than a game. It was subject to the legislation of governing bodies. It became of multinational importance. Increasingly it seemed to have inbuilt moral and commercial implications. It commanded recognition and patronage on the highest educational, political, and diplomatic levels.

There are other facts which are worth considering at this point.

*Since the so-called purge of August 1971, when the administrators of the Football League took it upon themselves to clean up the game, and many players suffered severe penalties for alleged misdemeanours, the subject of rough play was on everyone's lips. The media went hysterical and the whole consensus was that rough play was a characteristic of the modern footballer taken in from the 'permissive society'.*

But complaints about dirty play have been there right from the start. So awful was the conduct of footballers at Eton College in 1827 that the game was banned for ten years – a longer period of disgrace than suffered by any club in modern times!

Compare this with the fate of Leeds and Aston Villa in our own day, who not long ago were publicly humiliated by the findings of an FA disciplinary committee. And then relate such incidents to the writing of an 'Old Stager' in 1887. He was certainly one who had enjoyed the privileges of higher education and supposed social superiority. He said:

. . . in our time we played for fun, and we enjoyed the rough and tumble of a manly sport. Now, your footballers go into training for their matches, wear shin-guards to save their legs, and with all their skills have taken all the rough and tumble out of the game.

In this connection there is a story about Lord Kinnaird, once President of the FA and – to be truthful – a great influence for good in the way in which he fostered the game on every level. A fearless footballer himself, his wife once expressed the fear that he might be brought home with a broken leg. A friend assured her that if any leg were broken it would not be that of her robust husband!

Concerning his Lordship this anecdote is generally taken to be creditable, because, naturally, he was a gentleman. But if told about any one of a handful of modern players – to take a couple say, Nobby Stiles or Norman Hunter – it would be intended merely to bring discredit. There are, of course, plenty of other examples of double standard judgment outside of football.

Many people will say that a modern player 'reacts to the crowd', suggesting that what happens on the field reflects behaviour on the universal Kop. For safety's sake these people also suggest that the crowd also mirrors the on-field behaviour. Without saying more about this directly at this point we may take another backward glance; this time at crowd behaviour at two matches, one in Scotland, the other in England.

In 1876 a Scottish crowd – mostly supporters of Queen's Park – rioted when their favourites unexpectedly marred an unblemished record for the season by losing in a cup-tie. In 1888 Aston Villa played Preston North End in a cup match in Birmingham. So great was the disorder caused by factions in the crowd that the assistance of the military had to be invoked! And these were not isolated examples by any means.

Class distinction, feelings of regional, or metropolitan superiority, envy and plain prejudice affected the game early on. In 1884 Blackburn Rovers went to London as Cup finalists and their supporters were described by the *Pall Mall Gazette* as a 'northern horde of uncouth garb and strange oaths ... like a tribe of Soudanese Arabs let loose'. It would have been difficult to have been more offensive. But northern excellence rankled. Blackburn teams had appeared in three successive Finals, winning the trophy twice.

What one must not lose sight of in the middle of all this activity is the players who made the game, and for whom (in another sense) it was being made. By the 1880s there were hundreds, indeed thousands, of players belonging to teams of varying degrees of prominence or obscurity, all over Britain. Many young men played (as they still do) for the love of the game. Some said that they did this but were nevertheless not unmindful of the fact that football (like rowing or cricket for a much smaller minority) could aid advancement in business, in a profession, in the armed forces, or in society. Then there were those for whom football seemed to offer a way out of deprivation – at least for a time – and a means of asserting individuality.

The starting-point for football was, of course, the club. In the early days, because of experience in organization, access to expertise in drawing up constitutions and so on, and an unconscious desire to 'unionize' effectively in all fields, the effective football clubs were connected with public schools and universities. The army, the Civil Service, and a few clubs based on business associations dominated the scene in the early phases of the game. The main influence came from the south; a rivalry between north and south is still a major factor in football.

Partly through the influence of southern devotees of the game, partly through adaptations of already existing football traditions, and partly through the instigation of greater local pride because of additional recognition in local government, substantial northern football clubs came into being. There were even powerful local Football Associations, one of which, Sheffield, was powerful enough for a time to dare to challenge the authority of London. But in the end, for better or worse, there was a general acquiescence in the final authority of the FA.

In 1863 the FA had been the fulfilment of the wishes of young men. Forty years later some of these young men were still in commanding positions – but no longer young. This was the case throughout the County associations. The situation is hardly any different today. In a paternalistic era this did not matter – or did not seem to matter – as much as it does today. Nor did the fact that individual clubs came under the control of the kind of people who proved most able to perpetuate their own traditions. The best of these traditions, perhaps, was service to the community. The worst of them centred on an assumed right to tell other people what to do.

Football clubs represented groups either wielding or wanting influence and prestige. A League match, even more a Cup match, a hundred years ago was a kind of shop window (like the Boat Race and other prestige sporting occasions), and crowds were drawn to watch them in ever increasing numbers. A hundred years ago gates of 10 000 were not all that uncommon. In 1901 the Cup Final between Sheffield United and Spurs at the Crystal Palace was watched by 111 815, a record up to then. (That match was drawn and Spurs won the replay at Bolton).

It is more than interesting to look back and to discover how some of our predecessors looked into the future. It was about 1905 when an unnamed humorist wrote an *Extract from the Rules of Football, Year 1950*. He laid down that

the field of play shall be surrounded on all sides by wire netting on iron bars . . . to prevent spectators encroaching on the field . . . in order to argue with the referee; all clubs should provide a coat of bullet-proof armour, to be worn by the referee, and a clock which automatically takes the time off when a player is hurt, or the referee is turning a man off the field . . .

From one angle we might suggest that this writer misdirected his shots which do, however, find a target with phenomenal accuracy in, say, an Italian or South American setting. This is in spite of what some professional pessimists say about British football.

In his *Association Football*, 1907, William Pickford (who was, in turn, player, referee, journalist, and member of the FA Council!) forecast a British Cup, at which 500 000 spectators would attend. These would come from all parts of Britain in 'air motors, great and small, electro-plated, red-cushioned, swift and noiseless' to an arena with its own air motor arrival depot, with tier upon tier of seats as comfortable as those of a West End theatre. The players would perform not on grass but on a special surface of rubber ('grass is quite gone out of fashion'). The referee would be earning (remember this was written seventy years ago!) £3000 a year and would be appointed by the Football Committee of State, a department of the Civil Service. The game, opined Pickford, would be 'taken away from the acrimony of conflicting Leagues and Associations', and controlled by the State; ' . . . Football and indeed all games had been taken in hand entirely by the Government, and were run for the people and by the people', and supported by a special tax. And what about players in this dream world? 'Players are classed and paid by the State.

The top class receive £2000 (in today's terms say £20 000) a year each, and so on down to £200 (£2000) a year.' Misdemeanours on the field were to be referred to a Punitive Committee of the Football Department, with a tariff of fines at their disposal.

Some of what purported to be a light-hearted look into the future reads with startling accuracy. Whatever else may be said about Pickford's views he had some regard to the worth of a player, if only in monetary terms. As far back in time as that few other people did. There might be professionals, but they were not to be regarded as belonging to a profession. If only there were a Pickford today in the corridors of football power!

*... I now know differently, having spent the last nine years trying to improve the conditions, welfare, and last but not least the image of the modern professional footballer.*

# 2. The Beginning of Professionalism

*'There was a time when I would not tell people what my profession was. But over the last decade things have changed about being a professional footballer. . . .'*

The professional is not an amateur, and the amateur is not a professional. Anyone who makes his living through an art is counted a professional, whereas anyone who practises it in a dilettante way is regarded as an amateur. In sport we have a similar contrast between those for whom any branch of sport offers a livelihood and those who take part in it simply for pleasure. There is much more that could be said about what is a profession; but these simple statements of fact lead us into the subject.

What has so far been said does not arouse any emotion. But when we go one stage further we find that few subjects arouse more emotion. For a long time, indeed, 'professional' was a special kind of dirty word. That it still is in some quarters we learn when we look at some people's reactions.

The views of the rugby football authorities on professionalism in sport are well known. Whether sufficient attention is paid on the highest level to the supposedly true principle of what is amateur is another matter. However, there is hardly any discrimination as intense as that directed at a rugby footballer who puts his talents at the disposal of a rugby league club in the north.

It is not long ago since amateur tennis players earned as much as would support an entire Fourth Division football club for a whole season. Making honest men and women of some of them at least cost such an effort that the Lawn Tennis Associations of the world are still reeling with exhaustion – and a strong sense of compromised virtue. Within living memory nominally amateur cricketers (W. G. Grace was honest enough to admit to the existence of inducements) used one dressing-room and one gate onto the field while the professionals who made the existence of that sort of amateur possible were compelled to use another dressing-room and another gate. At one time the professional cricketer addressed his amateur captain as 'Sir' – a habit carried over to the playing-fields of public schools where old county players acting as coaches in their later years were expected to address the smallest and youngest of their pupils in the same way. In the heyday of the soccer amateur – now far out of sight – there was a similar division. On international duty amateurs who were selected were segregated into first-class railway compartments.

*As a matter of fact, it is worth noting the hang-over from this exercise of class distinction on the railway. It is not very long ago since the directors of one very famous club and their entourage went on one train, and the team and their assistants on another. Officially no doubt this was based on the prerogative of royalty that in case of sudden death by transport disaster not all should be lost. Though it is difficult to see what value there would be in the survival of directors if the players of a team were lost! In respect of another team – Wolves – the end of an era was brought about by simple forgetfulness. British Rail forgot to reserve the usual second-class compartment for the team on one occasion, so we had to spread ourselves all over the train – which was not very convenient. After that it was much more sensible to travel in first-class reserved accommodation altogether.*

Old habits die hard. The amateur of the old school no longer exists in the active sense, but the spirit lingers on, exercising a somewhat negative influence. The old style amateur of the C. B. Fry type (in our contention no absolute amateur, unaware of the fact that even for the purest there were rewards to be reaped from athletic achievement) was high up on the social listing. Where, in contrast, does the averagely good professional footballer stand in esteem today? He may be a professional, but he is not considered in any way a member of a profession.

B

*The fight to achieve a proper recognition has gone on for a hundred years. It has been a hard fight.*

*One has only to look back on the careers of footballers. Many once famous players, and at the head of the profession, now only live in a kind of twilight world, without recognition and often in real hardship. For a very long time the proper end of a player was thought to be in a pub. To be a landlord was a fitting sort of honour. (In the United States, sportsmen appear on university and college 'rolls of fame' and are even given honorary degrees!) Otherwise the frugal player who had spent little and saved hard was, perhaps, able to set up a newspaper business in a side street. For the rest there was a choice between low-grade factory work or unemployment.*

That gives some idea of the anxieties of a footballer's life and the inevitable sense of insecurity that dogged him in the past. The insecurity remains even today, but it is made all the greater by other pressures – pressures from which most other people are free, but of which they need to be made aware.

From start to finish the footballer must be prepared to submit to ruthless tests which in a crude manner determine which of the fittest shall survive. The 'competitive society' is a fine idea – so long as you are not involved in the competition! A footballer must regulate his private life so that his physical condition (in season at least) is never far from perfection. He must submit to hearing, or reading, frequently ill-informed, sometimes offensive, and – not seldom – quite fictitious accounts of his family circumstances, financial status, and mental state. He may be destroyed by a single sentence from an unfriendly commentator. It is known that the confidence of international players of great ability has been frequently undermined by ill-thought observations and seemingly malicious patter. One can extend this observation to include as victim Sir Alf Ramsey. A footballer is not allowed to fail. Failure spells quick decline and certain oblivion.

There is a cant phrase which goes the political rounds. Soliciting for votes, the politician shamelessly states: 'I am the servant of the public!' It is the professional footballer who may more truthfully come out with this, knowing that because of the fickleness of the public whose servant literally he is he may through no fault of his own find himself out in the cold. The public is not only a fickle master, it is a bad master – to the extent that in this field it exercises tyrannical powers. Here we may instance the case of George Best.

This matter of tyrannical powers is heavily underlined by the behaviour of the public. One does not need to have played for Celtic against Racing Club of Argentine at Montevideo, nor for Ipswich against Lazio in Rome to understand what the public can do. In comparison with those in South America and Italy, crowds in Britain appear almost models of good conduct – though the media will have one believe differently. But, even so, it is more than depressing to play under stress – of personal worry, family cares, lost form – before any home crowd suffering disappointment, or an away crowd looking for an Aunt Sally. To be singled out as the villain of the piece, and subjected to continual verbal abuse and malignant comments in the board-room about which one hears only long afterwards, when they have taken effect, is no pleasant afternoon or evening out.

The football field, of course, is an arena where all sorts of psychological disorders to which human beings are subject are liable to erupt. This is so obvious that it should not need pointing out. Unfortunately it is so obvious that virtually everyone misses the point. The best way of understanding this matter of tension is to think about one's own emotions during a game whether as player or spectator. The lesson is that one should try to think of oneself in the other man's shoes.

The football club as an organization is a mirror of social ideas. Because it is concerned with a game it must take notice of the ideas which lie behind and within the concept of a game, even when this is professionalized. There is, for example, the idea, even the basic idea, of fair play. Whether observed or not through its activities the club organization must be held accountable to the fair play principle, and so must the player, and so must the referee . . . A football club in Britain is also a business concern, based on the general principle of independence which hinges on the pivot of success. The commercial urge, as things are, has to be strong. Whether this can be compatible with the idea of fair play is for the reader to think about and find his own answer.

*What must not be forgotten is that at the centre of all this is the player. The player is a person, not a machine, and as such unpredictable.*

*The modern theologians of the game, trained in the seminary of Lilleshall, try to defy this truth and to turn players into robots.*

Many questions are asked about football today in many quarters and by many different kinds of authority. This is acknowledgement of the importance of the game. Many questions are raised concerning footballers. What concerns us is whether they are the right questions, and whether they are asked in the right way, and by the right people.

It is a hundred years since the basic questions concerning the status and living conditions of the professional footballer began to be asked. At that time life was easier, in that some were supposed to be entitled to ask the questions, others only to answer them when called upon to do so. The Victorian world was divided into masters and men, and the men did what the masters told them, mostly without even thinking of asking questions. The masters – this word meant practically anyone who was an employer, or an administrator, or merely well off – were favoured by having authority on their side. Church and State then clearly decreed where obedience should lie.

In an old book on football one chapter is headed, 'The insidious advance of the Scottish "professor".' The reference is to the number of skilful Scottish footballers who became members of certain northern clubs. That came about in this way. Employment prospects were brighter in industrial England than in Scotland and (as had been the case for a long time already) many young Scots sought their fortune in Lancashire and Yorkshire. Not that they thought in terms of fortunes; it was enough to be able to subsist. Skill in football was a recommendation to some employers, in the first place particularly in Darwen, Sheffield and Preston.

In the short term this would not have mattered very much

if the supremacy of the gentlemen of the south had not been challenged. (The north-south conflict already hinted at on p. 13 is built into the history of football as it is in other departments of national life.) In 1879 Darwen F.C. reached the Fourth Round of the FA Cup. They were drawn to play against the Old Etonians. To do so they had to make the long trip to London. Indeed, since the match ended in a draw they had to make a second trip south rather than their opponents coming north. This surely suggests a modicum of prejudice. The only way the Darwen club could undertake its commitment was through public subscriptions and charity. In modern times we sadly find British athletes also having to rely on charity disguised as sponsorship.

The Old Etonians went on to win the Cup in 1879, but the writing was on the wall. The working lads of Darwen, coming straight from the factory, and even after an unconscionably long working week, were endowed with skills which only required proper nurture to achieve results at least as good as those of the then best.

The gentlemen of the southern clubs enjoyed facilities for football unknown in northern England – though not in Scotland so far as the Queen's Park Club was concerned. They could easily take time off from work (if, indeed, they even needed to work) when it might be prudent to do so. They could afford the expense of playing. They could eat well, whereas few members of the northern working class could do so. They were, in short, at an advantage at every point. Moreover it was in the early days of football they and their representatives who ran the administrative side of football.

When the north made a spurt and came in for some of the spoils (see p. 12) the southerners did not like it. They complained that the northerners were professionals.

Professionalism was an established fact before it was discovered, so to speak. What affected the final issue was the matter of definition. In 1877 the once famous Heeley club of Sheffield contained two players whose names were on everyone's lips – Jimmy Lang and Peter Andrews. Lang had been well known to Sheffield enthusiasts before he left his native Glasgow, for on several occasions he had played for the combined Glasgow team against the combined Sheffield team (matches between cities which anticipated the Fairs, later UEFA, Competition). His own clubs were Clydesdale and Third Lanark. Andrews was even more widely known, for he had been a member of the Scottish national team in 1875. Sheffield football already was much indebted to a local manufacturer, Walter Fernehough. The debt was increased in 1877 when Fernehough gave a job in his works to Jimmy Lang, and when another manufacturer did the same for Andrews. At about the same time two stalwarts from Partick Thistle, James Love and Fergus Suter, turned up in Lancashire football, as members of the Darwen team.

Darwen made the mistake of drawing attention to themselves by reason of their success in 1879. The desire of a rich man with a love of football to perpetuate his name by establishing a great team is not unknown at the present time. One need only instance the rise of Coventry City, and the debt owed to one man, Derrick Robbins. Ninety years ago the biggest patron of the game was William Sudell, an executive in a cotton mill in Preston. He decided that Preston should have a fine team. In carrying out his intention – with enormous success – he blew all the fuses in the higher realms of football administration and politics. Sudell induced no fewer than eight of the best Scots to form the nucleus of Preston North End. There is no doubt that they came south primarily to play football for a living. Work in the mills was a nominal occupation. Looking outside of Britain today one can see exact parallels to this, in respect of the professional amateurs (see p. 10) who dominate the soccer section of the Olympic Games.

In the 1870s one or two of the local Football Associations had looked at the professionalism that by now everybody knew existed but of which there was no positive proof. On one occasion the Lancashire FA suspended the Accrington club. The Birmingham Association disqualified one or two players. But the rules were very vague.

When Sheffield Wednesday borrowed three players from Derby for a cup-tie it was only thought improper by the team against whom they were playing. And complaint was only registered because the Wednesday won! Their club officials blandly excused themselves by simply saying that they 'did not start the system of borrowing players'.

*It is ironical that nearly a hundred years later (in 1973, in fact) the Football League was still being caught up in conflicting ideas about the ethics of borrowing, and this in spite of long experience and supposedly cast-iron regulations. There was a proposal to loan Tommy Smith, the English International and Liverpool captain, to Stoke City. At the time Stoke City were very hard hit by injuries. Liverpool were happy to be able to help Stoke – who had made it known that they were looking out for players to strengthen their staff – and the player had indicated his willingness to take part in the arrangement. There was, however, a clause in the agreement that Smith could be recalled to Liverpool instantly if the need should arise. This it was that caused the whole plan to be defeated, even though it was perfectly within the letter of the law. The official Football League statement said that although there was nothing illegal the kind of contract invoked was not designed for this kind of circumstance.*

Another doubtful practice that came to light in Sheffield in the 1870s showed how very light amateurism could be on the moral side. Wesley College was attended by some students who were very good footballers and it had a fine team. That is, it had a fine team if all its members turned up! But on important occasions they were often absent. Wesley College lost one cup-tie against Heeley because nine of its first team stars were absent playing for other clubs which could offer them some inducement.

It seems incredible that something like this state of affairs should have prevailed a century later. And this is why something had to be done to correct the behaviour of amateurs who were in no respect deserving of that title.

In the *Football Annual* of 1880 C. W. Alcock, who was one of the founders of modern football, wrote: 'There is no use to disguise the speedy approach of time when the subject of professional players will require the earnest attention of those on whom devolves the management of Association football.' A committee was set up to investigate the matter, but it did not seem that this or any other committee would achieve anything.

The crunch came on 19 January 1884, when Preston North End played Upton Park (now West Ham) in a cup-tie at Preston. After a drawn game the London club laid a protest before the Football Association. To general surprise Sudell came clean. He admitted that Preston players were paid, and pointed out that this was the case in respect of many clubs and many players. At this Alcock, Honorary Secretary of the FA, realized that radical measures would need to be taken to save the game and to assure its future. He put up a proposal that 'professionalism be legalized' and asked that it should be considered at a special meeting of the FA. It is extraordinary that as far back as then the FA was regarded with awe; it was, said one writer, an 'old and able body . . . which has shown itself capable of dealing with every problem'. Perhaps, after coping with the crisis that confronted it then the Association deserves the compliment.

But Alcock's proposal had a long way to go before the green light was given. The die-hards in the FA were convinced that professionalism was evil – and this was the exact word used. They began throwing rules around with abandon. If a player lost wages to play for a club, he could have wages made up but only for one day in a week. In cup-ties only Englishmen were to be allowed to play for English clubs. Regarding other matches, 'foreigners' (i.e. Scots, Irish, or Welsh) must fill in forms to show their occupations before coming to England, their jobs since migration, their wages on each side of the divide, and their reasons for wishing to change their place of residence. Those used to filling in visa applications today would manage to reply to such a questionnaire without difficulty. In 1884 it was different. The forms went unfilled. Angry officials of Lancashire clubs threatened to form a new body, a British Football Association, in order to remove the game from the unrealities of the conservatives who looked like getting their own way.

In the early 1970s the Football League similarly threatened a breakaway from the FA over the issue of discipline which, it was felt, the more conservative body had left among the 'unrealities'.

During the first six months of 1885 the debate went on, and numerous meetings were held by the FA to try to reach a final conclusion. Although the southern amateurs put up a strong opposition to professionalism there were even more vehement opponents elsewhere – especially in Sheffield and Nottingham, centres of amateur zeal in England, and in the Scottish FA. On 20 July 1885, however, the champions of professionalism gained a notable victory. At a special general meeting of the FA it was decided by a majority of thirty-five to five to legalize the payment of players.

At the beginning of the next season, 1885–6, a new rule began – 'Professionals shall be allowed to compete in all Cups, County and Inter-Association matches . . .' after which followed the necessary qualifications. Irksome though these things were they did not obscure the main principle, and in the course of time they were to be altered.

The first professionals in football were simple men to whom all the subtleties of argument were meaningless. They liked playing football. They were good at playing football. They had otherwise no chances of escaping from anonymous drudgery. Why should football be reserved for the playboys of the middle and upper classes? When professionalism became legal life became a little easier for the administrators. Players, however, found that not all was honey. They were subject to the severe disciplines that ruled the commercial world of the nineteenth century.

More than this, they were written off as agents of moral decline. One writer was delighted that the evil of professionalism had at last been contained behind a frontier: 'so far the legalization of the "bastard" had only affected the North and Midlands'. Of course, spectators were well pleased to be able to see better football and in no sense disappointed that the FA Cup Final became dominated by professional clubs. But 'however much one might follow with delight the career of the big professional clubs, it was with a sort of feeling that it was something low and debasing, and that professionalism once introduced into the South would ruin the game, and the idea was pretty general'.

It is not likely that many professionals read that – which is as well. They might have said what they felt they ought to say, and that would not have made for better relationships. Pessi-

mists are always around, with a perpetual belief that whatever
is is wrong. Come 1887, and more football matches are being
played. So – 'Lately . . . and especially since every match
between good clubs has been able to draw a good "gate", the
footballers, especially the professionals, prolong the game into a
spurious summer season. Now football is essentially a pastime
for the winter, summer football neither conduces to good
play nor to *bona fide* sport, and we hope speedily to hear of its
abandonment.'

*Even twenty years ago British football was entirely a winter game,
and players had a more than three-month break. Many players, indeed,
turned to county cricket during this long break in order to make a living
wage. Now we are living in the jet age the top-class footballer virtually
all the year round endures football on different continents.*

*For myself, I have not had a break since 1965.*

In the first years of Cup and League football, in which the
foundations not only of British but of world football were laid,
it was the hard-working professionals who really did the spade-
work. They were the craftsmen and the artists and they
deserved if not precedence then at least proper recognition.
Pickford, whom we have already met, thought so. In his
*Association Football* of 1907 we read these words, which still
have a ring of truth:

In one respect at least the professional was superior to one section
of the players, that which might be called, as it has been styled so
often, the 'Shamateur'. Though it has now for twenty years been
made lawful in football for players to receive payment for their
services, and though the highest honours have been showered upon
the ablest of them, there still exists a certain amount of pseudo-
amateurism which perhaps owes its existence mainly to false ideas
of the social inferiority of a man who is known and registered as a
professional, and partly to the persistence with which in some
quarters the 'Act of 1885' [legalizing professionalism, see p. 25]
has been refused local sanction.

The following paragraph from *The Observer* of 18 November
1973 shows again how the attempt to retain amateur status
at all costs leads to a declaration against which Pickford's

strictures of seventy years ago are apt. It is the kind of wanting it both ways shown below that suggests a higher degree of basic integrity in true professionalism in sport:

Three cheers for honesty in a Press release from GKN Distributors Ltd., Fasteners and Hardware Division, concerning Britain's amateur 10 000 metres runner David Black: 'His terms of employment remain the same as when he joined Davis and Timmins at the invitation of chairman, Mr E. B. M. Grubb – a full-time salary for part-time work to remove any financial strain while he pursues his career in athletics.

*. . . There are still many class barriers to overcome, but a few of us have managed to go through them.*

# 3. Organization of an Industry

*'What is the role of the individual within a football club?'*

A football club is an institution in British life. This is because of the history of the game, which has brought many individual clubs – and by no means only the famous ones – through decade after decade as a firm point of reference in the social structure. A football club in Britain harnesses loyalties as no other body does, for it concerns virtually everyone. The excitement and enthusiasm in Sunderland in 1973 when, after many long years in the wilderness, the local team won the FA Cup in a decisive manner, was unbelievable. The whole town, and the whole of the north-east region, joined together in rejoicing. At least, it was thought, people far off 'down south' know where Sunderland is and that it has its own identity.

It is fair to say that there is no country in the world – even those where football reaches a high degree of excellence – where there could be anything comparable to the Sunderland situation. And this situation potentially exists in eighty or ninety places where there are League teams.

At the other end of the scale there is the overall sense of gloom that can envelop a town when things are going badly on the football front. It may show a lack of sense of proportion (or it may not), but the simple fact of Manchester United being relegated causes more feeling of outrage than the devaluation of sterling.

There is a very good reason for this. The football situation is one that is real, substantial, local, and at once understandable. It was not for nothing that football a long time ago was described as 'the simplest game'.

For a player in a team in decline the idea of calamity is a very real one – because he has to take the rap. A supporter knows (or thinks he knows) where to pin the blame. In the other matter of failing money power he is not aware of the long-term effect, and even if he were he would never be able to shout his protest at the people responsible. There is a recent example of the way in which football issues become larger than life issues.

*On 29 April 1972, the Quarter Final of the Nations Cup, England v West Germany, took place. Everyone looked forward to seeing this live on* TV, *since the two previous meetings between the two countries had been breathtaking spectacles. There had been the 1966 World Cup Final, decided by a goal about which the arguments still run on; and the 1970 World Cup Quarter Final, which was determined by Mueller's goal in extra time. The promised third encounter was obviously of great national interest to both countries, and from all points of view. But the British fans very nearly did not see the match live, because it took so long for the* FA *and Football League to settle their own differences as to the size of the fee acceptable from the* TV *authorities. What determined the case in the end was public feeling funnelled through the newspapers. This is the kind of case about which people will turn out with passion* **to** *take part in a referendum. Whether they would for other national matters of much greater intrinsic importance may be doubted.*

Charles Dickens put the difference between happiness and misery in this way: 'Annual income twenty pounds, annual expenditure nineteen nineteen six, result happiness. Annual income twenty pounds, annual expenditure twenty pounds ought and six, result misery.' There are plenty of Micawbers in football! A striker, in a team solely for his scoring power, has one chance in an important match and hits the right side of a goal-post – result happiness. On the other hand, he hits the wrong side of the post – result misery! That is the story of the English team in recent times. The margin of allowable error is a very slender one.

A single mistake in a match has incalculable consequences. So far as a club team involved in a European competition is concerned, it can result in the loss of anything up to £100 000. Failure to qualify for the World Cup means a loss of revenue right up the line, from the player who will do no more than sit on the substitutes' bench to the government whose coffers stand to benefit in many ways. It is a truism to say that football is big business. But it must be stated again, for it is a very big business indeed. And who runs it? In many cases the same sort of people who were in control a hundred years ago.

In a way this is understandable, even though it leaves much to be desired. The foundation of the industry in Britain is the club, and the industry itself can never really be stronger than is allowed by the separate bodies that constitute it. This has never been more apparent than today, when there seems a general uncertainty about where we are all going.

*There is no doubt about this, that the football club serves the community. If we look at this on the purely local level we are entitled to ask what other inexpensive entertainment is there to compare with it. Attendances are down on what they once were (which will be dealt with in detail later on), but an awful lot of people go to watch football matches in the course of a season. Add to these all the millions who switch on football matches on* TV *and the total of spectatorship is awesome. The World Cup Final of 1970 between Brazil and Italy in Mexico had more people watching it than had the first men setting foot on the moon.*

The reason for such a state of affairs is that football is an entirely human activity and an intelligible one which shows basic ideas and conflicts in dramatic form. Scientific achievement is, it seems, less praiseworthy than once it was. For one thing, the way science is applied too often leads to a process of dehumanization. Man is squashed out of his universe by the machine. We have even reached the point where nature itself can be destroyed by science. Football, in its own way, is at the very opposite pole. Its centre is physical action as an expression of emotional conflict. People who take part in football matches, whether as players or spectators, do themselves a great deal of good by getting rid of pent-up emotions. There is no doubt at all that in this way football has a definitely therapeutic value, even though there may be another side to be considered.

One of the strengths of football is that it has done so much to serve the needs of the underprivileged in our society. As a public spectacle it began its great development among the working classes, and it did an immense amount of good in giving colour and meaning to the lives of the poor. It also offered a way of life to those who wanted to use such skills as they had to escape from the prison of the back streets of industrial society in the nineteenth and early twentieth centuries. Football not only served the poorer in the community, it was served by them. Clubs survived on the gate-money of thousands who willingly stood in all kinds of weather to watch their local heroes. The cloth cap image may be a joke to some, but they should take notice that it is part of the tradition of football of which those who have the interests of the game at heart should be proud.

We are now, perhaps, getting rid of the cloth cap image. This is partly because the game has become respectable – through TV and because of its international connections, but partly because cloth caps are out of fashion. Society has changed, but one cannot say that football has kept pace with change in all respects. The inability always to keep up with change is most easily noticed in some – the majority in fact – of grounds. The modern word (although it is a very old word) is stadium. Whenever a team is abroad it plays in a stadium. So far as we are concerned at home there are very few places where one can describe the football ground as a stadium with any degree of confidence. For many of us there is no need to do more than walk down the road to see how little the local club ground has changed in half a century. That there will have to be radical alterations is clear from government legislation; but how to achieve them is another matter.

Lord Wheatley's Report into Crowd Safety at Sports Grounds, published in May 1972, provided invaluable information on the subject, but laid the whole cost of making improvements to bring grounds up to the standard demanded by more stringent regulations on the sports bodies themselves. In the case of football it was suggested, and this was endorsed by the Government Minister responsible for sport, that clubs could make provisions for the necessary work by economizing in other directions. All this has been under constant scrutiny, with the clubs asking the more urgently for more money to come out of the pools which can only exist because of the clubs.

We are brought back to the matter of direction.

Football clubs in England came into being more or less casually. Hundreds of them were formed in the first few years after the game became official. The records of the FA Cup will show some names which are not now familiar but which once had a place of honour both nationally and locally. This is the real crux of the matter – locality.

Most societies within the community develop because of the energy of a small number of genuine enthusiasts. These are the people who make it their hobby to form committees. The first organizers of football clubs were natural committee-men. They were, according to the terms of reference of the period, 'leaders'. Leadership, as it was understood, was interpreted according to established, if unspoken, rules – out of which came various 'establishments'. These rules tended to confirm the same sort of men (women had no part in the game!) in a self-perpetuating football oligarchy which, however, showed itself publicly as democratically inspired and elected. It is small wonder that the word 'establishment' has come to have a special meaning, which does not always encourage confidence.

Leadership, as it was understood, was determined by the fulfilment of one of three conditions: the possession of a proper pedigree, membership of a recognizably respectable profession, and industrial or commercial eminence, of which a lot of money was the best evidence.

The place of Lord Kinnaird in football has already been referred to. He went on to be a member of the FA Council and after that its Treasurer and its President. He did a great deal of good for the game, for he was a good deal more democratic than some others who wielded influence and had no inhibitions about professionalism when that topic was introduced into debate. Nevertheless, being a Lord was no disadvantage; it meant that he was automatically looked up to. The pattern of patronage from aristocratic quarters (note the reference to Kinnaird on p. 119) was widespread. Patronage from the same direction, for what it is worth in any practical sense, is still to be found – not least in the FA Council. Among the Honorary Vice-Presidents there is a fine collection of coronets (if not kind hearts) belonging to an ermined pack of Dukes, Earls, Viscounts and Barons, not to mention Right Honourables and Knights!

*All the nobility and the other 'right' people – legislators, administrators, and so on – who are the establishment of football are to be seen at what is their Annual General Meeting – the Cup Final.*

*There is no reason to complain about this anachronism, unless one feels that the contribution made to the most democratic of games by such persons is less than considerable. It is, however, fair to point out that it is difficult to find names of former professional footballers among the top brass in football administration and patronage. It is also fair to ask, why not? This question will be gone into in depth a little later.*

In the early days of aristocratic influence there was one special channel for its operation – through the public schools. Boys who played football at public schools helped to set up football clubs outside. A. N. Hornby was at school at Malvern and he was one of those who helped to establish Blackburn Rovers. The Kay family who were in at the start of Bolton Wanderers were pupils at Harrow. C. W. Alcock, who was the originator of the FA Cup competition, was also a Harrovian.

Medicine, the Church, and schoolmastering once provided the major part of the middle-class backing for football. Queen Victoria's own physician on the Isle of Wight, Dr Hoffmeister, founded a football club at Cowes. At Southampton one of the early presidents of the club and architect of its early successes was a well-known practitioner – Dr E. H. Stancombe. The present Chairman of the Council of the FA belongs to the medical profession. He is Sir Andrew Stephen, whose name will otherwise go down to posterity as being (so far) the only Scot to hold the chairman's office in the FA.

Many doctors had a dual interest in football. They had opportunity to practise their skills on a variety of patients, and to indulge their own personal interests. In the course of time a number of club doctors were taken onto boards of directors.

The Church of England monitored much of the social development of the last century. It is not surprising that it was an effective agent in sponsoring football – particularly as its aristo-

C

cratic and public school associations were strong. Some of the moral urges that ebb and flow within the game and within the consciousness of some of the journalists who often take the players to task sprang from this source. To the Victorian parson life was a kind of football game – but fouls sometimes seem to have escaped notice! Many clubs had the clergy somewhere in attendance, and sometimes very eminent ones. For instance Bishop Wilberforce, when he was an Archdeacon, was also President of the Southampton Club. In the last few years the Bishops of Coventry and Norwich have made themselves known outside their own circles by their keenness for their respective football clubs.

Schoolmasters, whose standing was greater in former times simply because there were not so many who reached their standard of education, came into the game somewhat under the influence of the clergy – who had their hands firmly on public education. Schoolmasters (who provided some good players in their time) could always be relied upon to do a lot of the hard work! Within the history of the clubs there is a fine record of work by schoolmasters. At Bolton the line of teachers active at board level stretched across a hundred years from the legendary W. T. Dixon to H. T. Tyldesley. On another level the game as a whole, and the professional game in particular, owes much to the schoolmasters who founded and have continued to run schoolboy football in both regional and national organizations. At this stage it is pleasant to be able to record that there are some schoolmasters who have gone into that profession from football.

As far as commerce and industry were concerned, interest was twofold. There was a genuine love of the game itself – which was shared by every other male in the community at a time when it was almost the only source of general entertainment. But there was also a shrewd idea that football could pay off in terms of prestige. Considering who else patronized football, the rising business men saw benefits in associating with them.

The story of the larger and older clubs in respect of origin is much the same – only the names change. There were tycoons on Wearside long ago, and some of them made the first era of greatness of Sunderland. Robert Thompson and James Marr were shipbuilders. Samuel Tyzack was a coal owner. They put money into the club, and invested some of their profits in Scottish footballers – still a principal export trade so far as North Britain is concerned – and they engaged a secretary who was something of a genius in his own right.

It is worth noticing that although the Sunderland team consisted largely of Scots in the 1880s and '90s there were some fine local players. One of these was Arnold Davison, an outside right who was for a long time a popular local hero. But he died in 1910, forgotten and unsung, in a Sunderland workhouse. Nor was he the only professional footballer to have suffered such a tragic end: when the cheering stops, today's hero becomes tomorrow's forgotten man.

The Football League was formed in 1888, by which time the game at top level was dominated by skilled professional players. What with that and the intense rivalry in the Cup competition – not to mention the then great interest in local competitions and even friendly matches – it was small wonder that football was increasingly pulled into the commercial ambit. Under the Companies Acts, 1862–93, all large professional football clubs became limited companies. All but one, that is, for Nottingham Forest remained, as it still remains, a club controlled by a committee.

Transformation to a limited company naturally altered the relationship between employer and employee, if only at first in a marginal way. For the responsibilities of both parties became matters of closer definition and stricter control. In the long run the development of the relationship between the two parties has been influenced by happenings in the wider sphere of industrial affairs in general. This, however, is not as fully realized as it should be. The Press seems sometimes to have one set of values for itself and another for other people when industrial relations are concerned.

Certainly the Press does not always appear quite impartial when considering the rights of footballers as employees. Often, in fact, there are outbreaks of hysteria when players begin to look even like mentioning their rights. Not long ago journalists were disrupting the provincial papers by selective industrial action. At the same time the players of one famous team, bereft of a manager in a manner that did no one much credit, nearly (the operative word!) took a mild form of protest by suggesting stopping training! About half of hell was let loose on the theme of players' duties, responsibilities, and so on . . . Outside the industry of football the idea of paternalism is practically defunct. Inside it, this is by no means the case.

Nothing illustrates this better than the comment of a very distinguished football journalist, Geoffrey Green of *The Times*, on the case in point. Remember that the directors – manager row referred to was in no way due to the players. Yet being innocent parties they were greeted with this barrage of condescension: 'All is supposed to be sweet and light at last as the . . . players apparently come to their senses after behaving like children in search of a lost nursemaid . . . Now that the players have apparently come to their senses . . .'

It is worth while looking back to a typical 'Memorandum of Association', the document by which a limited company football club was brought into being. The objects for which such a company was formed were various, and potentially beneficial in a wider rather than narrower sense. Broader possibilities are hinted at. For instance, a club was empowered to promote all kinds of athletic functions according to its constitution. It existed in order to help 'the physical being and development of the human frame'. It could undertake the business of 'restaurant proprietor'. It could purchase, alter and 'improve' the buildings it acquired. In short, a football club's charter existed very much in the public interest.

The public interest can mean several things. To the average fan the public interest element in his favourite club means him and his friends. He argues (and has always argued) that he pays the bills in the long run through his regular gate-money. When anything goes wrong the fans demonstrate, people write letters to the newspapers, and citizens in general feel a sense of involvement. When a club is doing badly businesses complain of lack of trade. In the more precise sense, though, the public interest means only the interest of the shareholders.

It was not long ago when the director of one club put this

quite clearly. He was asked by the representative of a foreign team what were the duties of directors, and what particular department of the club's activities he personally was responsible for. He thought for quite a long time, and then said that his duties were to look after the interests of the shareholders. A perfectly correct answer, if more than a little limited. But it goes to show the difference between present and the distant past.

In 1893 Arsenal wanted a new ground. First their landlord at the Invicta Ground on which they had played proposed putting up their rent. Second they needed a place suitable to their new status as members of the Football League, Division Two. So the directors launched an appeal for supporters to take up the shares that were being made available for the establishment of the new limited company. These supporters rallied round splendidly and £4000 worth of shares were subscribed. But directors and keen shareholders alike saw their duty as taking them further. They set to at weekends and in the evenings to help in putting up stands, dressing-rooms, and creating terraces. In those days the realities were nearer at hand.

The first directors of the clubs were for the most part solid citizens. Those of the first board of Sheffield United, for example, included two chartered accountants, three solicitors, two manufacturers, one retail merchant, and a surgeon. (The last-named was a son of a football player of earlier days in the city.) These people, with a sense of idealism that has largely been lost, put money of their own into the game. If they were not able to do that they helped in other ways, as has been shown. In provincial towns directors of football clubs were frequently town councillors. It was because of this and because of the prestige attached to a town through a successful football team that municipal interests quickened. Mayors and Corporations boasted of their teams. They still do. But too often that is where real interest ends.

It may be that both local and national government has a great part to play in developing our game. This will be done, however, only if it is lifted out of the category of 'cottage industry'. In earlier times directors of clubs were prepared to put their shoulders to the wheel. Gradually their influence was eaten away by their own frequent negligence and by their shoving everything onto the manager.

*I remember being involved in a conversation with a director which carried on into the early hours of the morning; he kept on insisting that he got nothing out of his investment in the game. I did not want to hurt his feelings by pointing out that he was getting a great trip with all expenses paid, staying in the best hotels, spending money – £10 a day.*

*To be a director one only needs to hold a small number of shares, although this varies according to circumstances.*

In the old days the average director was a small business man. The football club lifted him up, gave him business contacts that were useful, and a platform. He could speak from this platform with some sense of authority. The present-day tycoon director feels it the same way, with the extra bonus of publicity. The tycoon doesn't really mind whether the publicity he receives is good or bad; to him all publicity is good, which certainly is not the case with the player, without whom in any case no one else would be able to get any publicity. This being so it is obvious that players (often without their knowledge, and certainly without their consent) have been made use of to further the interests of others.

It is often said that politics and sport don't mix. A true story shows that this was not always accepted, and also how players could be exploited. In 1910 the Chairman of Middlesbrough was a Colonel T. Gibson Poole, an ambitious and ruthless character who was a Conservative candidate for Parliament. The election was to take place on 5 December, two days after a local Derby between Middlesbrough and an all-conquering Sunderland. Over the previous week the Middlesbrough players had been instructed to go out canvassing and speaking for their Chairman. When Saturday came Poole had another bright idea. He sent the club manager into the Sunderland dressing-room with £30, which he was told to offer to the Sunderland captain to divide with his colleagues on the understanding that they would throw the match. Victory for Middlesbrough, it was reckoned, would bring out the Colonel's supporters in large numbers. In the event the Sunderland captain properly reported the facts to his manager and directors. The Middlesbrough team played above their record and won the match deservedly. The Colonel lost his election. The Sunderland club reported the whole case to the FA who held a Commission of Inquiry which resulted in Gibson Poole being thrown out of football altogether. No doubt he felt hard done by.

There are plenty of people today who say – and write – that the ethics and morals of the professional game as we know it have declined and are now at rock bottom. These are people who not only will not look at facts but seem only anxious to destroy. What happened in Middlesbrough in 1910 certainly would not be possible today. A contemporary director would not dare to assume the right assumed by T. Gibson Poole, to treat players – whether his own or of another club – as his personal property.

*One wonders today, however, what some businesses would be like if they were run on the same haphazard lines as most football clubs still are. The amateur director has been kicked out of most industrial and commercial board-rooms. But not in football. The board meets formally maybe once a week, once a fortnight, once a month. More often if there are major financial problems. These may increase, if only because the economic climate makes money expensive and bankers less inclined to put further credit at the disposal of those whose expertise more and more lacks credibility.*

*The decline in directors' actual powers went side by side with the growing dominance of the secretary – often the 'grey eminence' of football. One does not need to draw attention to the considerable power exercised at times by the secretaries of the Football Association and the Football League. So far as clubs are concerned it may seem that the secretary is somewhere in the background. But his influence is powerful. One reads about managers being sacked, but never of the same fate befalling secretaries. Whatever other changes take place, the secretary of a club stays on. A quick-change sequence of decline and fall, and revival, would see a quick-change sequence of managers. In the case of a secretary, however, it would seem that he is as the Rock of Gibraltar, there for all time, and sometimes almost into eternity.*

In the beginning directors did the donkey work. Then they hired men to do the job for them. 'Besides possessing great educational ability, the secretary should be a gentleman of good position, with whom distant officials would not deem it derogatory to correspond.' That was the advertisement for the first secretary of Sheffield Wednesday, and it is very interesting to compare it with the advertisement put out in 1973 in respect of the post of Secretary to the FA. Taking into account the great changes that have taken place in the intervening years it is possible to notice a certain similarity in the required qualities. Part of the 1973 advertisement read: 'A man of standing is required to direct major new developments. Preferably, he must be broadly experienced in business administration and international negotiations, at or near the apex of commerce, industry or in government.' The Sheffield Wednesday directors of a century ago would have understood the language and approved the secretarial image.

The secretary's function was somewhere between those of adviser and dictator – according to personality. The first great club secretary was Tom Watson who constructed Sunderland's 'team of all the talents' after he had been persuaded to Wearside from Tyneside. Watson ruled both players and directors with a rod of iron. He, of course, was secretary and manager. The dual office continued for some time until there was a division of duties and large clubs had, as now, both secretary and manager. Whichever way it was, their importance increased inversely to that of the directors. At the present time there is no doubt as to who is cock o' the walk, and that is the manager. On this subject Frank McGhee wrote as follows in the *Daily Mirror*:

Doesn't it all strike you as slightly strange that so much attention has been paid to managers recently? Isn't it rather odd that the movements, actions, reactions and opinions of managers seem to be taking preference over the performance of players?

And doesn't it make you wonder whether, basically, this is one of the many things wrong with the game at the moment?

*It doesn't strike me as odd. Before the last war there were only a very few managers whose names were well known. After the war there were*

# A FLIGHT OF FANCY.

## WILL IT COME TO THIS?

'A Flight of Fancy', cartoon from *Sheffield Star*, c. 1930

Left: Professional footballer, old-style (1893)

Below: John Richards and Derek Dougan, professional footballers, new style (1973)

Right: First-class football, old style; Sheffield Wednesday v Preston North End, January 1893

Bottom right: First-class football, new style; Wolves v Ferencvaros (Hungary), U.E.F.A. Cup, 1972

Above: Serving the community I; finding a lost ball at Dromore, Co. Down, c. 1950

Below: Serving the community II; Saturday afternoon on a minor league ground in Cheshire, c. 1950

*still only a few prominent managers – Stan Cullis, Arthur Rowe, Matt Busby, for instance. Then we come on to the 1960s and emerging from that period, among others, were Don Revie, Bill Shankly, Joe Mercer, Bill Nicholson, and Jock Stein. They became household names through the success of their teams – a point which needs emphasizing. No more proof of this is needed than the knighthood given to Alf Ramsey in 1966. He would be the first to say that this was earned by the England players.*

*After seventeen years and six English clubs I have reached this con-clusion: whatever role in a club an individual plays, from chairman down to the youngest apprentice, it is to him the one that is absolutely vital!*

# 4. Organizing a Union

*'The more things change the more they
remain the same'*

It is significant that in the definitive four-volume *Association
Football*, published in 1960, every organization within the game
and every aspect of the game were discussed in great detail,
with one exception. This was the emergence and significance
of the Professional Footballers' Association.

It is not that the PFA (or its predecessor) was not mentioned.
It was, but in such a way that it would have been better served
by omission. There were about two sentences (in Vol. I, p. 8,
and Vol. II, p. 313) about a body which deserved considerably
more notice on historical grounds alone. What other large-
scale industry is there, one might ask, of which the employees'
association would be so peremptorily dismissed?

This kind of treatment is symptomatic. For it has so often
seemed that the last people to be entitled to a say in the running
of their affairs have been professional sportsmen. The same
attitude has prevailed throughout. In cricket, racing, and now
in tennis and athletics, as well as in football, there are those in
authority who presume to know best. It is a convenient myth
that top-class athletes are amateurs. But it is only a myth.
As far as organization – which is what is under discussion here –
is concerned, the celebrated runner or jumper is not more free
from direction than a properly professional sportsman. In
amateur sport which has the proper credentials, of course,
matters are dealt with on a democratic basis, with each
member of a body entitled to express his views without fear of
being discriminated against for having done so.

At the time of writing a group of gentlemen, somewhere in,
or approaching, their seventies, are setting out to see how the
famous Chester report of 1968 can be applied to football. This
report came to many sensible conclusions, not the least of which
dealt with the need to give professional players a right to voice

opinions in the higher councils of the game. The Report seemed so sensible in respect of so many things that it was put on ice for five years. When at last it was taken off it was sent not to the people most concerned with its practicability but to the supposedly wise men of the game. It is as remarkable as it is true that many of the main issues in Chester were being tossed around sixty years before!

It took a relatively long time for professional players to discover how they could join together for the protection of their interests, and we are still suffering because of this. The prime reason was the fact of the 'cottage industry' nature of football in its earlier phases. Out of this came the determination of club directors and Association and League administrators that players should be kept in the place to which it had pleased God to call them. The idea that a football club was a co-operative venture in which some invested money, some expertise, some enthusiasm, and some (the players) technical skills and know-how, but in which all were entitled to be regarded as equal, would have been considered seditious at one time. It would not be generally accepted as a workable foundation today. So it is that directors and managers – the gaffers and the bosses – and players – the workers – remain in the same relative stations.

As soon as professionalism was legalized, however, it was inevitable that there should be calls for the protection of players' interests, if only because of movements towards greater security among the working class from which all the professionals came. In the early days there was not much money to argue about. The receipts of Bury F.C., for instance, for 1885 amounted to £140, out of which £105 was paid over in players' wages. At least this does not point to any undue wastage on the side of administrative costs! A year later the wage bill of Bolton Wanderers was no more than £15 in any one week. The Sunderland 'team of all the talents' was worth 25 shillings per man per week. But success, and a desire not to lose talent, prompted a rise so that players were soon on a rate of £3 all the year round. In 1893 the Football League tried, but failed, to establish a maximum wage of £140 per annum. All of that sounds a long way off. But one aspect of the remuneration of those times is not so remote. For also in 1893 a signing-on bonus of £10 became statutory. This bonus (now called a signing-on fee) stayed at £10 until only a few years ago. It was then doubled. Whether £20 today is anywhere near £10 of eighty years ago is open to doubt.

As the game became more and more popular, more money came into it. By 1896 the season's takings at Bury were £4987, out of which a little over half went in players' wages. During this period, as has been described, most clubs changed their constitutions, and their new status as limited companies gave an impetus to the more politically alert among the players to consider the advantages of unionization. In 1870 compulsory education had been introduced into Britain. A year later the Trade Union Act gave formal recognition, that had hitherto been lacking, to this movement. The great period of expansion of trade unionism was during the last decade of the century. This was when a greater degree of literacy began to become apparent among the working class, and also when football entered its first era of industrialization.

In 1898 the idea of a National Union of Players took shape, and in the next year such a body was constituted. Not altogether surprisingly it was virtually impossible to find any club with directors who seemed to be prepared to give even moral support to such a scheme. A clause in the proposed constitution of the new body gave as one of the aims the protection of members against 'adverse legislation' by the Football Association and the Football League. Neither of these authorities was pleased. The senior of the two, the FA, 'promptly set its heel on the same'. It indicated its firm belief in its own infallibility because of its ability to settle all matters in dispute. 'Invocation of the law to settle disputes', it loftily preached, 'should be a last resort.'

All the controlling authorities – Associations, League, and the clubs – noted to themselves that, by playing their cards right they could defeat the threat of a Union. There had not up to that time been any effective organization to develop the will towards solidarity among the rank and file of the players.

The main subject for debate among players at the end of the last century was wages, and argument about the justice, or injustice, of imposing wage restraint through maximum wage legislation went on for a long time. In 1900 W. Heath of the Staffordshire FA moved that a maximum wage of £4 a week should become operative at the end of that season. But no sooner had this been agreed on than some of the more ambitious clubs felt that they were being held back for the sake of the lame ducks. A prominent campaigner for the abolition of the maximum wage was F. W. Rinder of Aston Villa. Rinder was a man of ideas and vision, who would seem a big man today. He was by profession a surveyor. Having been largely responsible for the early rise to fame of the Villa through his initiative, administrative ability and ruthlessness, he took it badly when his plans were thwarted. He looked a long way ahead, and he envisaged a super-stadium for Birmingham able to hold at least 130 000 spectators. He drew the sketch plans for the stadium himself, but there was more of nervousness than optimism about the viability of such a scheme, and it never came to pass. Rinder, who was exceptional in appreciating the players' point of view and in supporting their collective aims, also drew up proposals concerning wages, and the FA Council set up a committee to prepare a report in the 1903–4 season.

This committee came up with a compromise proposal, that there should be a sliding wage scale. But the FA, having called for the report, turned a deaf ear to its conclusions. Reports that urge change in the existing state of affairs often suffer this fate.

On 30 May 1908, the matter of wages was again before the FA Council, and a piquant situation developed when J. C. Clegg of Sheffield was preparing to move the abolition of restrictions on wages and bonuses. This would have been entirely to the liking of the players, of course.

Because Lord Kinnaird was absent his place in the chair was taken by Charles Crump of Wolverhampton. Crump was a member of the Birmingham FA, and also a member of the main FA Council. Clegg pointed out that since it was well known that in certain instances the existing regulations were being ignored it would be as well to dispense with them. The spokesman for the opposing point of view was T. H. Sidney of Wolves, who said that the system was working well enough as it was, and that it ensured that the less wealthy clubs (such as his own) would not be deprived of the opportunity of competing on reasonable terms with their rich neighbours. If there were no wage limits the few rich clubs would monopolize the best players. In this way success would breed success. 'Everything in football,' said Sidney, 'must not be sacrificed for money.'

The debate was won by the adherents to the Sidney philosophy, which exerted a strong influence for a long time to come. The kind of ideas expressed about footballers and a minimum or maximum wage were, and are, of more general origin. Football itself is a symbol and most of its operations also are symbolic. There should be no surprise, then, if people talked in 1952 as they had done fifty years earlier.

In 1952 a Committee of Investigation was brought into being by the Ministry of Labour to examine the football industry. The Players Union (as it still was) proposed a new type of contract – no wage ceiling, contracts for less than one season (i.e. a trial basis agreement), or alternatively one for three years or longer, and no restrictions on transfers when contracts had ended. The League and the FA united, as they had done before, and protested that any change in respect of players' terms of employment would not be in the best interests of the game. There is a favourite saying, often given out by the media when short of something of substance to say, that 'the game is greater than anything or anybody'. Like many other grand utterances, this does not stand close examination. In application, however, it frequently works to the disadvantages of the profession – it is the same argument as that which leaves artists dying in poverty. The irony in the present connection is that the players are the game.

The 1952 committee agreed with the authorities and stated how 'richer clubs would undoubtedly be at an advantage in the competition for players' if the maximum wage clause were to be revoked. They went on to say how 'star players would tend to be concentrated with a few rich clubs, and thus the general standard of League football would decline'.

It is bewildering that in the Chester Report the same conclusions were again being reached, so that 'the tendency has been for the best playing talent to flow to a few already successful clubs, thus guaranteeing their continuing success'. The irony here is that, as things have worked out, the relaxations that have come into contracts have not had quite the expected result. Some rich clubs have fallen badly from grace, and the more they have spent the further they have fallen! But the world has taken quite a liking for say, the likes of Ipswich, Burnley, and Queen's Park Rangers.

In the early battles for contractual freedom there were casualties. Of these the chief was the Players' Union. By 1905 it existed only in some meagre funds protected by a Mr Cameron. Several things, however, conspired together to make the revival of the Union both desirable and necessary. The FA had itself been incorporated under the Companies Acts 'in order to facilitate the carrying out of its objects'. Transfer fees had rocketed and when Alf Common was transferred from Sunderland to Middlesbrough for £1000 in 1905 the whole football world was shaken. The love of money, as is tritely said, is the root of all evil. St Paul's saying is applied to the game today, it was also applied in Alf Common's day. Then it was assumed that it was a matter which did not concern the footballer, even though he was the commodity for which sizable cheques changed hands. Alf Common's only claim to fame is that he was sold for a lot of money. When this began to be the criterion by which a professional was judged the amateurs went into a corner of their own and emerged in 1907 as members of an Amateur Football Association. It is another of the ironies of the game that in the end it is the amateurs who disintegrate because too many of them had been too ready to dispose of the principles which they formerly took as their distinction!

While all this was happening within football in the early years of the century, in the world outside there was a new climate of feeling and opinion that was by no means agreeable to most of the directors of most football clubs. It was a time when the rights of members of trade unions were under close scrutiny, and there was a good deal of militancy. In 1901 the judgment known as the Taff Vale decision, which was to prove a landmark in industrial history, had laid it down that trade union funds could be made liable for damage caused by a trade dispute. In consequence of this the Labour Party came officially into being, to win a number of seats in Parliament in the 1906 General Election. In this year the passing of a Trade Disputes Act by the Liberal administration of Sir Henry Campbell-Bannerman nullified the Taff Vale decision.

Although the first attempt to elect a body to represent the players' interests from among their number was frustrated, the idea was by no means lost sight of. It is a cheering thought to contemplate at times what may be achieved by the idealism of one individual who is prepared to stick to his guns. The key figure in the early days of the Players' Union was Charlie Roberts – whose career is a book in itself. The fame of Roberts is so far back in time that it is difficult to believe that he might still have been living, albeit in his early nineties.

As a player, Roberts was at the height of his fame just at the period which we are considering. He was born in Darlington, where he began his career as a footballer. From Darlington he was transferred to Grimsby, and there he became the dominating figure in the team, at centre-half. In the close season he used to work on a trawler in the North Sea and – presage of things later to happen in the fishing industry – slogged it out in the inhospitable waters off Iceland. Roberts believed that this annual experience on the high seas was a wonderful aid to fitness. Once he persuaded the Brentford goalkeeper Walter Whittaker to accompany him. Working among the trawlermen Roberts learned a great deal about human relationships, and about the necessity for proper collaboration and means of consultation within industry. From an obituary notice furnished by the then Secretary of the Players' Union (James Fay) at the Annual General Meeting on 21 August 1939 we can determine that Roberts as early as 1902 was actively engaged in trying to restore life to the defunct players' organization. But it was five years before his efforts were rewarded. In the meanwhile – at a fee of £400 – he joined Manchester United, and in 1905 played for England in all the three international matches. A colleague in the Manchester United side was Billy Meredith, one of the two or three most famous players of all time, and one whose dedication to a profession that released him from a lifetime in a Welsh coalmine – like that of Roberts – was lifelong.

Between them Meredith and Roberts drafted an invitation to their fellow professionals to attend a meeting to discuss the formation of 'an organization on trade union lines for the defence of players' interests'. This definition comes from the *Manchester Guardian* of 3 December 1907, which added the information that a Southern League club player named Mainman 'was carrying on a similar agitation in the South'. Within two years H. C. Mainman was playing for Notts County.

On 2 December 1907, the inaugural meeting of the new Players' Union commenced at 7 p.m. at the Imperial Hotel in Manchester, with Meredith in the Chair, and Roberts the power behind it. Almost all the players from the two Manchester clubs were present, and representatives of Preston, Sunderland, Newcastle, Blackburn, Sheffield United, Bury, West Bromwich Albion, Liverpool, Oldham Athletic, and Bradford Park Avenue. Letters of support came from players in these clubs: Derby County, Nottingham Forest, Notts County, Sheffield Wednesday, Aston Villa, Everton, Stoke, and Leeds City. All in all 500 players were directly or indirectly represented. For the time being C. R. L. Menzies took on the duties of secretary. After discussion the meeting agreed to set up a committee structure, to formulate a code of rules, and to communicate resolutions and intentions to colleagues in the south.

The report of this meeting in the *Manchester Guardian* indicates that some of the problems concerning players were among those that were still familiar until very recently:

Football players, like all other paid workers, have their grievances. Among the most skilful men, as among the directors of the wealthier clubs, there is widespread dislike of the rule which prevents the paying of more than £4 per week to any player. Such a rule, it is urged, puts a premium on mediocrity, and the recent levelling down of clubs is pointed to as proof of the statement. Players, as apart from club directors, have another grievance in the system which controls the transfer of men from one club to another. Under the existing system a player of any standing has the greatest difficulty in exchanging from one club to another, however valid may be his reasons for wishing to make a move. These are among the most knotty problems which the new Union will attempt to solve.

D

The fact that the Union was a revived organization rather than an entirely new body is attested by a note which confers upon the present PFA a kind of apostolic authority. This note, containing a resolution, simply says: 'Write to Mr Cameron for a statement of the accounts of the Old Union'. The capital letters in the end were inscribed by the then secretary.

The pioneers were both fast and efficient. The country was divided into sections for administrative purposes, the drafted rules were sent to clubs to be exhibited in dressing-rooms. On 14 December there was a further 'Open Meeting' and on 16 December, at the Charterhouse Hotel in London, the subscription for a player was set at fourpence per week through the playing season, after an entrance fee of five shillings. Further meetings followed on 23 December at the Maypole Hotel, Nottingham, and the King's Arms Hotel, Sheffield, on 27 January 1908. At this meeting a great deal was accomplished. The name of the organization was ratified as the Association Football Players' Union. The Presidency was conferred on J. H. Davies, a man of wealth who first rescued from disaster and then ruled Manchester United. The Vice-Presidents comprised Rev. J. Leighton and A. H. Briggs, both of Bradford, J. Cameron, J. A. Deacock, of Tottenham Hotspur, F. J. Walter, H. G. Norris, J. McKenna, of Liverpool, G. A. H. Catton, of the *Athletic News*, and F. W. Rinder, of the Villa, to whom reference has already been made. These men were, it seems, prepared to stand out against the majority of reactionaries who considered an organization such as the Players' Union subversive. Alas within a year their good intentions proved insufficient to stave off misfortune!

At this same meeting the secretary was instructed to get in touch with a parliamentary agent concerning the implications of the Workmen's Compensation Act of 1906, by which employers were held to be liable for accidents to their employers which occurred at the place or in the course of their employment.

Accidents, unemployment, insecurity; these were the spectres that haunted the professional footballers of those days. The fact that ordinary workers – the 'sturdy toilers' described by *The Times* as among the football crowds of the day –

suffered from similar fears made for a compatibility between players and rank and file spectators that diminished as the living conditions of many of the latter improved across the years. So it was that on 27 January 1908 the Secretary of the PU was told to ask permission from the FA for a match to be played, the proceeds of which should form the basis of a benevolent fund. At the beginning of April a resolution was passed that: 'a match be played between Manchester United the prospective League Champions (1st Division) and Newcastle United the Cup Finalists at Newcastle at a date to be mutually arranged between the two clubs, the proceeds to be devoted to the Benevolent Fund'. Later that same afternoon a meeting of the officers of the Union was held, and some revolutionary propositions emerged. The first was 'that a match be played annually for the benefit of the Union'. The second still awaits implementation. It took this form:

We, the undersigned being Professional Football Players registered with the FA respectfully request your Council to propose to the next annual meeting of your Association, that the Union be allowed to elect one representative to the Council of the FA, such representative to be a bona-fide member of the Union.

At the present time, during the 1970s, we are becoming aware of the 'points system' – a disincentive to unfair practices on the field which, to be truthful, is felt to be generally helpful. On 1 April 1908, Rinder moved, and Mainman seconded, a commendable resolution that was carried but never put into effect that:

It be permissible to the Directors of Clubs at their own discretion to award marks to their players for all matches during the season. Such marks being the reward of good conduct and skill . . . each mark, irrespective of result of match, shall have a money value of five shillings.

In 1908, despite the disapproval of FA and League, Manchester United and Newcastle played a match to raise money for a provident fund for the Players Union. The very term indicates the level on which these pioneer negotiators for players as a whole were operating. In 1949 another provident

fund was set up and in the Chester Report attention was drawn
to the unsatisfactory nature of this fund which was – even in
1968 – 'a relic of times when players were poorly paid'. The
match was duly played at Newcastle on 29 April and the
proceeds amounted to £182.15.9. The Union recorded its
gratitude to the Newcastle club for its cooperation and also
to J. H. Davies who had not only allowed Manchester United
to take part in the match but had also paid their expenses to
do so.

The affairs of the Union were now conducted with increasing
efficiency by H. C. Broomfield, secretary since 23 December
1907. At the end of April 1908 Broomfield's salary was settled
at £156 per annum. There was also a growing feeling of
militancy in the air due to a realization of the extent to which
players were exploited by the system and by the public. The
reasons for discontent are sometimes out of general view. So
it was in those days, but the mute facts on the minute-books
of the Players' Union tell their own story:

On 1 April 1908, the Secretary was instructed to ' . . . write to Sheffield United Club and ask them to increase the amount granted to
the parents of the late F. Levich "to an amount equal to what his
wages would have been for the remaining portion of the season" .'

The Union itself made a grant of £20 to Mrs Levich (presumably the mother) and called upon the FA to assist out of its
benevolent fund. The widow of the late George Smith, of
Southampton, was given £10. Later that year the management
committee of the PU considered other sad cases. F. Thompson,
of Norwich City, being in 'destitute circumstances' was awarded
£10. The case of W. Stagg, of Newcastle United, was under
investigation on account of his being 'in needy circumstances'.
A Bolton player formerly with Crystal Palace – W. Hall – had
made an appeal for assistance. It was recommended that his
case should be looked into also. If he was married, and 'in
absolute need' he should be granted £5; if unmarried, however,
there was to be nothing. Funds, after all, were limited.

The hazards of a profession for which there was inadequate
medical assistance, so that minor injuries untreated could
escalate tragically, in a time when death among the poorer

sections of the community was frequently accepted as according to divine dispensation, are reflected in a resolution proposed at the first A.G.M., at Ye Old Royal Restaurant, Birmingham, on 15 December 1908, by J. Sharp – of Everton and England – and seconded by Lindsay of Bury: 'That in the event of the death of a member, a levy of one shilling per member will be made, and the amount raised will be paid without deduction of any kind to his wife, or children, or nearest relative...' The end of that year was marked by fresh protestations on the part of the players on the subject of freedom of contract and on the related theme of professional dignity:

The Committee of the Players' Union feel that the time is opportune to affirm their conviction that the abolition of all restrictions on the financial relations of players with their clubs is the only satisfactory solution of the wages problem that clubs are faced with periodically...

(16 September 1908)

... free bargaining would cause the scandal of suspensions to cease, and save gentlemen of high social position the humiliation of being pilloried in the public press.

(A.G.M., 15 December 1908)

The Union by now comprised representatives of thirty clubs from the League, nineteen from the Southern League and one from the Lancashire Combination, and the headquarters were at 14 St Peter's Square, Manchester.

Very soon the leading members of the Union began to think in terms of militancy. According to the old West Bromwich and England player, Jesse Pennington, who was recollecting time past in old age, the international match between England and Scotland to have been played at Crystal Palace on 3 April 1909, was at risk. The match was to be played in the presence of the Prince of Wales (later George V), and it is said that the match was in doubt right up to kick-off time. 'I can tell you,' said Pennington, 'it was never the intention of any of the players who were selected to let the old country down. After the match Lord Kinnaird said the players who had taken part in the match would never be forgotten for their loyalty.' For the record England won 2–0. Jesse Pennington was, of course, there at the time, so one must accept what he says. Otherwise, the main evidence of the intention on the part of footballers to strike points to its maturing three months later.

One may note the words of Lord Kinnaird and wonder how long the thought of the players' 'loyalty' remained in mind. However this was, the FA did not like the look of things at all. Still less did they like the news that came down from Manchester after a meeting on 7 May 1909, at which Messrs J. Sharp of Everton and England, and a Lancashire cricketer, Meredith, Walter Bull, of Spurs, Andrew McCombie of Newcastle United, and a player named Craig agreed:

That the Union become affiliated at once to the General Federation of Trade Unions and that the following rule be inserted in the Rules of the Players' Union – 'If the Management Committee find it necessary at any time to withdraw from their employment, such members to be paid the sum of One Pound until [sic] they resume their occupation'.

The next stage brought direct confrontation between Union and Association, for the former took a case to court under the Workmen's Compensation Act because the latter 'had no rule dealing with the same'. The Council of the FA moved the suspension of the PU 'unless in future they obey the rules of the FA'. The ultimatum was set to expire on 17 May. Mainman, being chairman at the time, and Broomfield found it impossible to cope with a situation of such urgency during the close season, but indicated their own unwillingness to resign and their intention to soldier on at least until the A.G.M. which it was proposed to call in August.

Other members of the management committee resented bitterly the attitude of the FA, but felt obliged to resign their membership. However, on 28 August, some 200 players met in the Albion Hotel, Manchester, under the chairmanship of J. T. Jones, of the Municipal Employees' Association, and pledged loyalty to their Union. A resolution was passed, thanking the Manchester United players for the firmness they had shown. The United players had insisted on their right to be members of the Union and under the advocacy of Charlie Roberts, those who had resigned had rejoined. Many years later Billy Meredith recalled the great work done by Roberts at this time. It was, indeed, a time of considerable tension and feelings ran very high. The players were supported by the TUC. Arthur Henderson, a prominent politician, tried to help by proposing that matters should be taken to arbitration, an offer turned down by the FA. Two days before the 1909–10 season was due to begin there was complete deadlock. The players were prepared to withdraw their labour, and Manchester United intimated to their prospective opponents, Bradford City, that the match due on 1 September might very well not take place.

To avert the disaster of industrial action by the players a temporary truce had been called and the FA had made some concessions. The Players' Union was granted recognition; cases were to be allowed to be referred to the courts under the provisions of the Workmen's Compensation Act; all suspensions were to be removed; arrears of wages were to be restored.

The tensions within the Union were considerable. Compromise to some appeared as defeat. Broomfield went to the TUC asking what its attitude would be if the PU were to disaffiliate itself. He wrote to the clubs still in membership of the Union to ask for nominations for a new committee, and made a journey to Sheffield to talk to J. C. Clegg and to see if a *modus vivendi* (presumably including retention of the ties with the TUC) could be arrived at. He recorded that this meeting was useless. Members were balloted on the issue and, inevitably, a split occurred. However, at a meeting held in London on 2 November it was determined that the PU would no longer remain in membership of the TUC, hoping nonetheless that 'the FA will give the players their early attention so that we may have a steady settlement of the dispute'.

There was no steady settlement. But for the time being the FA felt the situation sufficiently stable to allow a minimum wage – of £208 per annum – to replace the previous maximum wage. The League, however, conveniently asserted its faith in the maximum wage.

*I am very proud of, and grateful to, the pioneers of earlier days.*

# 5. For the Good of the Cause

*'I am reminded of a famous wartime saying*
*by Churchill about the debt owed by the*
*many to the few'*

The dramatic events of 1909 led to a shake-up in the affairs of
the PU. It could have been that the organization would have
been completely eliminated, as was its predecessor. But some
strong-minded players had learned that unity offered the only
means of improving the lot of the general run of players. The
public is interested for the most part only in success stories.
Failure it rarely wishes to hear about, and certainly does not
often intend willingly to make provision for.

On 5 January 1910, A. S. Owen took over the secretarial
duties from Broomfield, and he was succeeded on 10 March
1913 by H. J. Newbould, who had had previous experience
as club secretary and manager. The Chairman at that time
was Colin Veitch, of Newcastle United. Charlie Roberts, who
by now had left Manchester United (from whom he received
a letter of thanks for his services to the club) for Oldham
Athletic, was still a conspicuous member of the management
committee, on which a prominent newcomer was James Fay.
Fay also represented Oldham Athletic for whom he had per-
formed one notable service on the field. In the season 1909–10
the team suffered only one defeat after the New Year and,
gaining thirty-six out of forty-two possible points, went into
the First Division hard on the heels of Manchester City. Fay,
centre forward, scored twenty-six goals in thirty-eight matches
that season. Schooled in Union matters at Oldham by Roberts,
Fay served the PU faithfully for many years. In 1929 he became
secretary and, carrying the affairs of the Union on in Southport
(where he had a sports business) during the Second World War,
handed over to Cliff Lloyd on 23 September 1953. The

administrative side of the PU (which became the PFA in 1961) was the more efficient because of the overlap of generations in office. For the last thirty years business has been the more smoothly transacted because of the presence in the office of Miss Hardman.

It was on the eve of the 1914–18 war that the Union achieved maturity. In the years between the wars it developed muscle. In the most recent phase it has acquired a reputation for statesmanship in that its opinions are sought in many matters which concern the relationship between sport and the public. There is no doubt that this progress in effectiveness and esteem has been due to a remarkable succession of officers, and also of purposeful player delegates.

In 1913 the new Secretary of the PU summed up what had been achieved in the first five years of the Union's existence. The achievement was not inconsiderable.

The rise in wages, the bonuses for draws and wins, and the part of a transfer fee negotiated for him, were advantages that came to the player only because of the persistence of the Union. Many instances of poverty and distress had been discovered and, although the Union's funds were limited, alleviated, while various cases had been contested in the courts. Above all, players felt that there was an authority to which they could bring grievances, and from which they could receive advice that was free of patronage.

One of the cases contested became a landmark in football history. In 1912 the Union fought a test case with the intention of upsetting the transfer system as it then existed. The transfer system was inherent in the original 1888 Rules of the Football League, but it had been amended so that by 1904 the FA had surrendered most of its prerogatives of control in this matter to the clubs and the League. The clubs, fearful of one another, stored up years of discontent by insisting on the 'power to retain' a player's registration beyond his agreed yearly service. The test case centred on events that were already past history. This is inevitably so – as witness the Eastham case of fifty years later. Supported by the Union an Aston Villa player, L. J. Kingaby, brought an action against the Villa 'for maliciously preventing him from obtaining employment as a footballer by keeping him on their retain list'. In 1909 three years after he had last played for the club he was placed on the open-to-transfer list at a then prohibitive fee of £350. When it had been argued in court, the case was withheld from the jury on points of law. The judge ruled that the plaintiff had no cause for action, although the fee required might appear to be excessive, since the defendants' action was justified by the terms of employment offered and there was no trace of malice. Aston Villa had gone into this action with the support of the League.

The Union Secretary did 'not criticize the learned judge ... but should have liked the matter decided by somebody who understood the working of professional football as well as the law'. However, by bringing this case the Union 'forced the facts concerning the transfer system before the legislators of the game, and before the public'. As a result of this action players were enabled to claim a share of transfer fees. The Football League acknowledged that clubs should no longer put un-realistic values on players whom they did not really wish to retain. Almost immediately after this case Blackburn Rovers gave intention of accepting the spirit of the Union's claim by giving free transfers to players whom they did not wish to retain. It is fair to say that when the Kingaby case was over the Football League acted towards the Players' Union with a generosity which the Union, having accumulated a large bill for costs, readily and gratefully acknowledged. At that time the Union had very little in the way of assets, and the legal costs of the Kingaby case alone amounted to £725.

Charlie Roberts served as Chairman of the Players' Union from 1913 until 1921, and was the key figure in the establish-ment of an effective organization. He was respected as a player and trusted as a man, both by his fellow-players and by management. He also had an instinctive grasp of negotiating techniques. At the meeting of the PU of 2 February 1921, he delivered a speech which is a model of its kind: simple, clear, and forceful:

We have called you here because the times are getting critical. We felt that it was time we had a meeting so that we might know where we stand and so that you might know from us how the Union stands, and what your Committee have done and are doing. We want you to realize that it is your Union. It is not ours. We are only your representatives. I do not want anyone here to be afraid to criticize us. Do not go back to your dressing-rooms and say what you have not said here tonight. Do not be afraid to speak. The time has come when we must go forward, we must try to improve the condition of our members. Some of you, no doubt, do not fully realize the difficulties we have in trying to get the smallest concessions for you. The League and the Football Association are very funny people to deal with, and we shall never be able to get much for you unless you stand loyally by us.

Players often say, 'What has the Union done for me?' We can only reply, 'What would you have been getting if it had not been for the Union?' If I were asked what you would have been getting but for your little Association, I would say that you would have been told that you played in wartime for nothing, and it might have been said, 'Why not give them two pounds and let them work? They will do it.' I believe they would have done something like that if it had not been for your Union.

If there is any man here who wants to know what the Union has done for him then I hope he will speak. We are here to answer questions, to hear criticism, and to place the position before you. We have some things to tell you which you would hardly credit. They show the way in which players are being treated today.

There followed a list of cases in which clubs had shed their promises in respect of players' rights in transfer deals. 'The Clubs themselves', observed Roberts, 'are one of the strongest Unions in this Country.' Next came a report on a libel action on behalf of one player against the *Daily Mail*, 'which tried to bluff us out of it. They said, "Go on, and we will make it costly".' Finally came news of a deputation which had gone to Somerset House and had managed to persuade the Inland Revenue to observe the provisions of a 1906 ruling that a professional footballer was (paradoxically!) a 'manual labourer'. This meant that they were (as the Inland Revenue had just said they were not) eligible for benefits under the National Health Insurance.

These were complicated and difficult issues, and Roberts stuck at them. But during 1921 he was appointed Manager of Oldham Athletic, which necessitated his retirement from the chairmanship. His fellow members in the Union felt it proper to mark his distinguished services on behalf of the whole profession. They presented him with a gold watch and (in the manner of those days) an Illuminated Address:

We, as representing the members of the Union, desire to place on record our grateful thanks and appreciation of the great services rendered by you, Sir, to the Professional Footballer Player. Ever since you assisted to found the Players' Union, you have worked with fearless and unselfish enthusiasm to further the objects which were its ambition.

We realize that you have made great sacrifices in the cause of the Professional Football Player whom you leave on your retirement from the Chairmanship, with many advantages, privileges and monetary benefits, which he did not possess when in 1913 you became the head of the Players' Union.

It was the desire of the Annual Meeting of the Club delegates for 1921, that your great services should be recognized, and that there should be written record of our appreciation.

The Chairman at that time was J. Lawrence, one time a goal-keeper with Manchester United, who spread the cause of football by practising for some time as a coach in Holland. Roberts had spoken of the power of the clubs. Players who took part in the activities of the Union were sometimes made uncomfortably aware of this power. They found themselves inexplicably being placed on the transfer list – for reasons unconnected with their playing performance. Those were days – as Vic Feather points out – in which a union official in any industry frequently found that many employers were unwilling to engage him.

This gives point to the Report of the PU secretary in 1932 – in a bleak period of unemployment and privation – in which he regretted 'that there are still players connected with some of the wealthier clubs who have not yet seen their way to join the Union, and yet are in a position to receive high wages, bonuses, benefits, etc.'. All these advantages, Fay (by now Secretary) pointed out, had come about only through the efforts of the Union. The League clubs at that time without representation on the Union were Arsenal, Everton, Aston Villa, Chelsea, Leeds United, Middlesbrough, Sunderland, Sheffield Wednesday, Sheffield United, Nottingham Forest, Port Vale, Swansea Town, Bournemouth, Brighton and Hove Albion, Clapton Orient, Newport County, Norwich City and Watford.

In the summer of 1932 some players in certain parts of the country who were unemployed found themselves denied unemployment benefit – on the grounds that they were seasonal workers – whereas unemployed players in other districts were not so discriminated against. The Union took the matter up at the highest level. They found Sir F. J. Wall, Secretary of the FA, a helpful ally, when it came to preparing a case and presenting evidence before the Umpire appointed by the Crown to deal with appeals concerning unemployment benefit. In the event the evidence presented to the Umpire on behalf of the Union was convincing and the right of unemployed players to receive benefits assured.

A continuing source of contention in the football industry was – and is – the transfer system. So far as the authorities have been concerned, despite palpable abuses, the 'retain and transfer' system commended itself largely because it existed. Whether it was just was another matter. Sir Charles Clegg was once opposed to the whole transfer apparatus. That was in 1898. Thirty years later he fell in line with the general run of administrators:

There is no necessity for me or anybody else to interfere with the arrangements regarding transfers. I do not think the present system is perfect, nor does any member of the Football League, but any criticism of it must be accompanied by suggestions for improvement. To say that players are under some system of slavery is perfect nonsense – nothing of the kind; clubs have to have some security at the end of the season to keep their players and it would be the height of folly to leave those clubs at the whim of the players. That is the only matter which in any degree can be described as slavery, and the Football Association is prepared to take the full responsibility of maintaining the system.

There are ways of loading an argument. Clegg did it by seeming to expose clubs to 'the whim of the players'. In 1933, speaking as Vice-President, Charlie Roberts urged the PU to express itself in the strongest terms 'against a [transfer] system that can take a living from a player'. The implications of that statement and the terms of the protest which emerged from the discussion following Roberts's remarks do not suggest that it was the players who were being unreasonable. This resolution went to the Football League Secretary:

That this meeting of Delegates of the Association Football Players' and Trainers' Union, strongly protests against the present Transfer System, which metes out to players very harsh and unfair treatment, causing many of them to go out of League Football, or to leave the country, and in certain cases preventing them from earning a living. It is un-English and out-of-date, and we earnestly request that the Management Committee of the Football League will receive a deputation from the ... Union at an early date to discuss the matter.

A request was sent to the FA simultaneously that it should also receive a deputation to discuss the application of Rule 31 (retaining fee) and the unsatisfactory manner in which it was generally interpreted.

Precisely nothing came out of these protests and the subsequent discussions. So that seven years later the Union committee and the management committee of the Football League could once again meet to 'discuss all the questions appertaining to the impossible and unfair position of many of the professional players under the rules as they stand at the present time'. Once again the Union pointed out that many players were being forced out of League football because of the excessive transfer fees being set on them. The authorities were relieved from having to take any remedial action (which was not intended anyway) by the outbreak of war.

At the Annual General Meeting of the Union on 21 August 1939 tribute was paid to Charlie Roberts and C. E. Sutcliffe, late President of the Football League, who were described as 'two of the most prominent men of their time, and probably ever, connected with this great game of Professional Football'. Roberts had spent thirty-seven years working for the well-being of professional footballers. 'I can assure you,' said James Fay, 'that if we had not had such men as the late Mr Roberts, I am

afraid there would not have been a Union today.' Billy Meredith, a trustee of the Union up to his death in 1958, spoke of
Roberts' 'great fight for the Union' and noted: 'He was recognized as one of the greatest players of his time, and sacrificed
honours to which all agreed he was entitled.'

At that same meeting it was reported how the secretary
had had an interview with the Chief Inspector of the (then)
Ministry of Education, and how an agreement had been
reached whereby players should be given opportunity during
their playing days to take courses which should fit them 'to
take their part in the commercial and business life of the
country when their playing days are at an end'.

Implementation of this scheme (which is now operational
under the direction of the PFA Education Officer, Bob Kerry)
was naturally held up by the war. At the outbreak of the
Second World War players' contracts were cancelled, and they
were unemployed. At the 30th A.G.M., held in Manchester
on 26 August 1940, a trustee in the place of Charlie Roberts
was welcomed. He was S. Sanderson, Secretary to the Card
and Blowing Room Operatives Association, and Provincial
Secretary of the National Association of Trade Union Approved
Societies. Speaking, he said, on behalf of one and a half
million trade unionists, Sanderson observed:

The great sport for the working man was football . . . After the
war they must be ready to at once function and ready to again
furnish the working man with his great sport of football. Considering the amount of money the game attracted, he was surprised
at the small amount which found its way to the pockets of the
players . . .

The next landmark in the process of remedying a situation
unsatisfactory to the professionals of football was the 1947
National Arbitration Tribunal. This led to some increase in
players' wages and to the setting up of a joint standing committee of FA, FL, and PU. But discussions of this committee proved
indeterminate and in due course the 1952 committee of investigation was brought into being – with little effect on the general
pattern of the football industry. Thereafter came the Eastham
case of 1963 – by far the most significant modern entry in the

record of the emancipation of the footballer – and the Chester Report. This document – after five or so years – is still on the table.

*I would have given almost anything to have played with Roberts, and under him as manager.*

# 6. Changing Forces in the Social Structure

*'I expect complete freedom for players within a year or two'*

There is more than a feeling in the air that dramatic changes will take place during the last quarter of the twentieth century. With unfailing optimism those who will not see it proclaim wonderful things to come in the twenty-first century. What will football be like then? There are plenty of prophets about, but we are concerned with the here and now, and the changes through which we are living. As usual the question is, who is changing what for whom? More than ever one is aware of the fact that people can be changed against their will, that there are manipulators about who have no scruples whatever, and that entertainers are in the forefront of those liable – for various reasons – to be changed. They are less likely to be with those who do the changing.

As we have already pointed out, football is a national concern whether we want it that way or not, because it is a national industry, and also a national advertisement; in short, an expression of the nation. In case anyone gets up to say how undignified, or even how disgraceful this is, it is worth mentioning that in some countries (indeed, in our own in previous times) the emblematic role played by football belongs to military departments, either openly or secretly. It has often and correctly been said that the conflicts within football are a sublimation of greater conflicts, and that this is one of its psychological functions.

But the national image part of this and the many implications make it all the harder for the front-runners, the PBI of the football machine, the players. They are, of course, told what to do, by fans, by non-fans, by press, by administrators, by politicians, and anyone else looking for an Aunt Sally. The same

E

goes for other entertainers – for artists, singers, novelists. And for similar reasons. They are part of the national image, and are held accountable in a way in which property speculators, or pools promotors, are not. The footballer gets done down for offences of the most sublime triviality – and his livelihood may be destroyed. A take-over specialist who puts hundreds out of work in pursuit of profitability probably collects a knighthood and a bucketful of praise.

When we go back into the story of football we see players who were in one respect much more free, in others much less free. Before the age of the manager, that is, before the second World War, the individual player on the field did what his instinct told him. So we have a gallery of immortals. Will Derby County ever have the peer of Steve Bloomer, or Arsenal of Alex James; Everton of Dixie Dean, or Stoke City of Stanley Matthews? These, it is said, were the great individual artists. But what did these masters earn, and how much economic freedom did they enjoy?

At the present time some footballers appear to be doing well. Here and there is one with a £20 000 mortgage, which entitles him to a nicely suburban residence, and a garage containing two motor cars, of which the real ownership lies still with the finance company that supplies the credit. To maintain the good life – as the colour supplements picture it – even the lucky player in the top football income bracket must do as he is told. In an acutely perceptive examination of himself and the game in general (in an interview published in *The Sunday Times*) Steve Heighway noted what the system does to the players and how, having known nothing else, the normal player accepts the system. This is hideously near to brain-washing:

I don't really want to go into the manipulation of people, but that's what it is. In other forms of management there is an attempt to handle each person in a different way. Football managers are untrained as managers, and they know only one method, total dedication . . . Managers don't worry that players can be totally destroyed by the time they're thirty. They don't care when you're ill, if you're on the treatment table, or when you're in the reserves . . .

Heighway said that footballers should be well enough paid

to be able to retire at the age of twenty-seven if they wish to, 'before', as he put it, 'the real humiliations begin'.

Looking at the present and towards the future reminds us that the state in which we are in at this time is the result of the enormous changes that have taken place in the last quarter-century. More precisely in the period since the end of the last war. As the war ended so did a six-year break in the pattern of British football. This break was to have more far-reaching consequences than the comparable break during the 1914–18 war. Life during the war was bleak, grey, colourless. And it stayed that way for some years. What football was played at that time was also bleak and colourless in that it was all rather unreal. Some of the great pre-war players went through the motions. They had little or no time for keeping themselves up to pitch and only minimal incentive club-wise. For years players had been 'guesting'. This meant that famous players from big clubs were playing in regional games in the north-east or the south-west, while obscure players from little-known clubs were regularly turning out in famous colours, according to the decrees of military service or industrial commitments in a society which had given up a large measure of individual freedom.

As soon as the League and FA Cup arrangements were restored football re-established itself and perfected its image. Or so it may now seem. Gates were enormous. One may look at some statistics. At the beginning of the 1948–9 season a local Derby at Goodison Park attracted a gate of 78 299. On a cold March day in 1950 Roker Park held 68 000 for the Sunderland–Newcastle match. In the seasons ending in 1950, '51, '52, '53 and '54, Arsenal home attendances averaged 49 000, 50 000, 51 000, 49 000 and 52 000. In 1956 66 655 went to see a cup-tie between Arsenal and Charlton, although by now the boom was really over. But in 1973, after England's elimination from the World Cup the average at Highbury was 35 000 – still pretty impressive! We may now look at some details of aggregate attendances at Football League matches. Pre-war, the average attendance was 28 million. In 1948–9 the corresponding figure was a little over 41 million. A season later one million spectators had disappeared. In the 1955–6 season the extent of the spectator drain is shown by an aggregate of 33 million. Today we are once more round about the 28 million mark, that is, almost exactly where we were before the war.

Large crowds, for whom comfort was minimal, used to represent a strong wish to escape from everyday drabness. They were also hazardous. It was not until the terrible disaster at Bolton in 1946, when thirty-three died and 500 were injured at a sixth round cup-tie against Stoke City, that the nature of the hazards became apparent to all. Of course, this was not the first such calamity. There had been a comparable roll of dead and wounded at Ibrox in 1901, and then again – believe it or not – at Ibrox in January 1971. It is worth remarking that in no other places of meeting or entertainment would safety regulations have been so pathetically inadequate. It may be, of course, that the working-class character of football in earlier days made it seem that the protection of its customers was less important than that of others in other places. To this day more is talked about than actually done. There was, for instance, a short debate in the House of Lords on 4 December 1973 in which a valiant part was played by Lord Wigg. But action still lags behind goodwill, and the recommendations of the Wheatley Report (see p. 147).

The post-war boom had other consequences. In some places clubs grew more ambitious than proper calculations would have recommended – given the existing conditions of control, management and finance. During recent seasons gates at Port Vale have been somewhere in the region of 3–4000. Twenty years ago there was optimism in the Vale boardroom. The old ground in Hanley was disposed of and a new one bought in Burslem. The idea was to have an enclosure second to none, with room for 50 000 spectators, and available to the community in general. The pity was that the Vale directors (whose ambitions led them to engage Stanley Matthews as manager) got their priorities wrong because their ideals were confused.

However, in 1953–4 all looked set fair at Vale Park. In the fifth round of the Cup there was a gate of 42 000 for the visit of Blackpool. The home team won and ultimately arrived at the semi-final, in which they just lost to West Bromwich Albion – the eventual Cup winners. Despite this disappointment the Vale won the Third Division (North) Championship and went into the Second Division. Three years later they were relegated – not to the Third Division, which now gave up northern and southern sections to provide a Fourth Division – but to the new lowest class. Quick promotion to Division Three was some balm to troubled spirits, but the zest which expressed itself in a new stadium had by now expired. How to operate in the public interest and how to work on a moderately profitable basis is the foundation of a successful first-class team. It was, and is, a daunting prospect without adequate public involvement and communal investment.

If one is critical of direction in the football industry one must also realize that many other industries have found the right answers to the wrong questions – or the wrong answers to the right questions.

U-turns have become all the rage! But football is always under the spotlight of public enthusiasm and exasperation, as the one subject on which everyone is authoritative. The very people who shout loudest – the fans, especially the fans who no longer actually go to football grounds, do not recognize that part of the problem of football in modern times is caused by their own way of living. After the war there was so little competition that football was bound to prosper. Gradually, however, living standards began to rise. New housing replaced old, but not in the same place – in the centre of battle-scarred industrial cities. Great new estates of flats and houses made new suburban areas, with less loyalty to the old city centre that had formerly been the focus of social activity. In the local sense, then, the downtown football ground seemed a lot further off. Especially on a wet and cold winter afternoon. The new houses were more comfortable than the old, and pride in maintaining them made additional calls on spare time.

The arrival of the five-day week coincided with the first phase of Women's Lib – except that it was not called that. The man of the house, freed from office or factory on Saturday morning now found himself doing, or helping to do, the family shopping. For this he had increasingly available his own private form of transport. The family car seemed only a blessing, but some of those who drove were frequently encouraged to take the family out for a ride, rather than go (as before) to that male reservation, the local football ground. The effect was felt even by the top clubs. For those in lower circles it was all but catastrophic. The 'little' clubs – some of which come up once every fifty years in the first round of the FA Cup – had their attendances decimated. So it remains.

There were and are, on the other hand, strong-minded football fans who, possessing cars, do not allow their interests to be obstructed. Motorborne fans reach major grounds each week. But there is a lot of picking and choosing. Accrington, Bradford Park Avenue, Gateshead, Barrow; these are recent casualties of the motor age. Poor facilities for spectators, poor teams, and the pull of more successful clubs within a radius of say, fifty miles, destroyed clubs that were once famous. This will be seen as the beginning of a long list of concerns that will have to reduce ambition. If the facts are assessed in the proper manner, that is, realistically, the end result may not be bad at all. But that also depends on new and vigorous approaches to the game as a whole – as a recreation as well as a spectacle – and to the connection of club with community in a much broader sense.

It is a paradox that football has been a victim of prosperity, but this is the case. Prosperity is a matter of how the national income is divided. When an adequate amount – relatively at least – is invested in any concern it will be able to live more or less comfortably. This is the continual gripe of those of us who are concerned about football in its entirety. An awful lot of people are making money out of the game – money which ought to be going back into it for the common good.

*What is euphemistically described by the ad-men as 'investment' sees, say, £160 million a year going into the pools, out of which the Government takes its share of over £70 million.*

*The end of the first period of post-war prosperity was surely marked by the coming of TV to such places as the depressed areas of Belfast. In 1952 there were few families without a radio. Four years later even the least affluent among the urban poor managed at least to rent a TV set. In modern terms it cost 40p a week. When father and son were both working they could manage half of the rental charge each!*

*There was a sudden rush of activity in the early 50s in respect of the new medium. Football was popular. The gates were still there for the taking, for the serious decline was yet to come. International football had extended its frontiers – because of the need to rebuild a shattered and splintered world – and the World Cup had acquired a new sheen. Flood-lighting was introduced, and this made all the difference.*

There had been experiments with primitive flood-lights far back in time. It was not until the great teams of the 1950s took the stage that flood-lighting became familiar. Again one has to draw attention to the suspicion which this innovation engendered. On 5 November 1955 Chris Buckley and Major Wilson Keys, chairmen of Aston Villa and West Bromwich Albion, declared themselves against the investment of £20 000 in flood-lights. (Harry Morris of Birmingham City, on the other hand, thought it a good idea as it would introduce continental teams to St Andrews.) Others, with a more plausible ground for criticism, suggested that if there was money to spare it should be invested in players. The best of clubs in fact produced their own players through their nurseries and home-based coaching facilities, and then had the teams that could effectively show to the world how effective and irresistible flood-lights were. The great Wolves team developed by Cullis which dominated English football throughout the 1950s had flair and their clashes with continental sides showed football at its dramatic best in an atmosphere made more theatrical by the lights.

Football under artificial lighting becomes at once more real and more fantastic. It truly is to be seen as a drama, and the ground becomes an arena, a stage. The dramatic element has been greatly strengthened by the wholesale transference of the game to TV. Radio commentaries on matches began in 1927. It is difficult to appreciate that some form of television coverage came only ten years later – a programme called 'Soccer at Arsenal', introduced by John Snagge and George Allison, being shown on 16 September 1937. However, the great changes that TV was to bring into the game only began to show themselves fifteen years later – for reasons already explained.

*The first major event to captivate millions rather than thousands was the 1954 World Cup, which took place in Switzerland. Twelve years and three World Cups later we find an astounding growth of interest in the game in general and the major competition in world football in particular. According to a reliable National Opinion Polls Ltd survey, in 1966 44 per cent of the population over the age of sixteen watched football with some regularity – i.e. at least once a week. During the World Cup competition two years later the viewing per-centage of the population for this event rose to 85. Even allowing for the most generous margin of error the figures are symptomatic of shifts of interest that have enormous consequences for those who play and those who organize football on the bread-and-butter level.*

TV has domesticated football. It is a fireside pastime for the great majority. And since this is the case it has been brought under a closer moral scrutiny. Almost certainly unfairly, for there is a vast difference in what is allowable in a game of intense physical energy on a muddy field in the way of ex-pression and in a drawing room. The screen makes some things look much worse (especially to women exposed to football for the first time!) than they are, and it also makes some things look much better.

It is late in the day to say that nothing is as truthful as reality. Football is played out of doors, on grass, under an open sky, and it is affected by wind and rain. One can get worked up when viewing a match on TV. That is undeniable. But the real and absolute sense of involvement (which leads the too enthu-siastic to run on the field at critical points) comes when one is actually there, with the advantage of the whole field being in view, with one's voice really having some effect.

There is a general opinion, however, that it is only on TV that the best can be seen – in sport at least. This opinion has a destructive side effect. Long years ago it was customary to decry everything British. The best music, for instance, came exclusively from Italy or Germany. We have now got into the state of believing that the best football comes from Brazil, or Yugoslavia, or Hungary, or Germany . . .

No one will deny that there are good teams in many countries, or that technical excellence is pretty widespread. It should be

Above: Chelsea v Arsenal, at Stamford Bridge; painting by
Charles Cundall, c. 1930

Below: Town and country; Molineux Grounds, Wolverhampton,
c. 1960

Leaders of men:

Top left: Lord Kinnaird, Football Association;
Top right: William McGregor, Founder of the Football League;
Above left: F. J. Wall, Secretary of the F.A.;
Above right: F. W. Rinder, Chairman of Aston Villa

Far top right: Palace revolution at Villa Park, old style; Rinder takes charge

Far right: Palace revolution at Villa Park, new style; Douglas Ellis (with H. Kartz and Tommy Doherty, Manager, left, and B. Mackay and H. Parkes, right) takes charge, December 1968

'Press' – the reporter's lot

said, however, that technical skill is not an end, but a means to an end. What the spectator wants to see is a good and exciting game, with movement and fire, and stirring moments of attack. A match between the two technically best equipped sides in the world can be intolerably dull. It is often asked who would want to go and watch two Division Three or Four teams on a wet February afternoon when all that is (supposed to be) best will be available on TV later in the day. The question is an unreal one. For football is so unpredictable. The best of the game for the spectator, and sometimes for the player, lies in its unexpectedness.

*When one talks about the unexpected, the sort of game that comes to mind is the one between Brighton and Bristol Rovers, at Goldstone Road, soon after Brian Clough's appointment as manager in 1973. The scoreline read 8–2 in Bristol's favour.*

*But TV tends to want predictability. 'Match of the Day' to those who do not think too deeply tends to suggest 'Best Match of the Day'. A lot of this is due to the setting: martial music to introduce and round off; star commentators and analysts who do a good deal of screen-hogging; and interviewing techniques (not only to be experienced in respect of football) which suggest that it is the commentators and analysts who are the true masters of the game.*

There are many dangers in this process. For instance, a player is booked at 3.30 in the afternoon for a misdemeanour. At 10.30 he is in a kind of Inquisition court, having to account for his action and to express proper penitence for his sins. Splendid viewing, but irritating, to say the least, for the player.

The theory is that TV provides the best. Therefore actuality is ignored, and the gate at Workington say, is 975. If this idea is the right one we should no doubt stay at home and glue our eyes all day long to the screen, where the best of everything may be presumed to exist. That, of course, is very nearly the state of affairs in the USA, and the results are not encouraging. For what should be the best is too often the worst.

The sleaziest thing that the TV age has produced is a kind of overheated romanticism. Romanticism in part consists of praising the past at the expense of the present. So far as football is concerned this divides into two parts. The English (but not the German, Brazilian, Yugoslavian . . .) game is at an all-time low. Never was it as bad as it is. Next, the game, such as it is, is without any real personalities. So people say.

*The great master of romantic fantasy is Michael Parkinson, who is to be seen everywhere in pontificating mood. Behind him lie the glories of football in Barnsley, upon which the sun no longer shines as once it did. Well, Barnsley won the FA Cup in 1912. But most of the time the club has existed modestly, and mostly in the Third Division, as a nursery for richer clubs.*

*Parkinson, the romantic, looks back as if still on the Barnsley terraces of long ago, thinking no doubt on what might have been but never was. Barnsley winning the League, the Cup for a second time, and then in Europe . . . Would Parkinson's criticism of the game today have been the same had Barnsley's achievement been greater than it was in his early days?*

*There is probably no one more sentimental and nostalgic than myself. I was going into the League Cup game with Tranmere [13 November 1973] and I was not only thinking about playing a team from another world. My mind kept drifting back to the numerous encounters against Ron Yeats [at this time player-manager at Tranmere] in the same world – Aston Villa v Liverpool, Leicester v Liverpool, Wolves v Liverpool. The two encounters – the draw at Prenton Park and the replay at Molineux – personified what English Cup football is all about. In a way, it was like David v Goliath, bearing in mind that David had already disposed of one Goliath [Arsenal] at Highbury. I was, truthfully, more than concerned with the tie, because if he could do it once he could do it again.*

*In the second game, which was closely fought – the dramatic winning goal came in the dying moments of the game – we had a 2–1 victory. After the game the Tranmere Chairman, Bill Bothwell, came in and said what wonderful sporting games between the two sides these had been. And the second display by the Tranmere team at Molineux was the finest he had ever seen from a Tranmere side.*

One is entitled to look back with affection, but this should not destroy the critical sense.

Almost certainly the average Third Division side of today is professionally more competent and without doubt much fitter than a team in the same class thirty years ago. For instance, on 8 December 1973, York City broke a forty-six-year record by reaching their eleventh League game without conceding a goal. On the same day, in the First Division, another Yorkshire side, Leeds United, equalled a twenty-four-year record set by Liverpool by going nineteen League matches without defeat. These are examples of real competence and real achievement, in a highly competitive setting.

The professional pessimists do no service to the game. But their influence runs through the Press. Boardrooms feel the cold wind of abuse. And players feel a great sense of frustration. Criticism is not resented when it comes from professionals who know what they are talking about. On the other hand when it is mere prejudice and part of a private image-building exercise it is.

This takes us to this other matter of the missing 'personalities of the game'. Football is essentially a team game and in the end what matters is the total effort of a team. A fine player fits in, makes moves, thinks ahead; the uninformed spectator may very well not see him at all during a game.

The TV age, however, requires a special kind of offering. What the viewer wants is not so much a personality as a sensation.

*There is not always a clear use of words in describing what a personality is. Often what people have meant here has been an individual who wants to go his own way. The so-called personality I have heard described by club officials from time to time as a luxury. I myself haven't escaped this comment. In fact, when I played for Portsmouth, Blackburn, and most certainly Aston Villa, my reputation was most definitely put in this category.*

Nowadays the TV audience seems to welcome the master of quick, cheeky repartee, even laced with occasional obscenities. This kind of personality, drawn out of almost anywhere in the world of entertainment, is not only welcomed but also regarded as authoritative on the economy, crises in the Middle East, law and order, or anything else in fashion on which he is invited to talk.

Every profession has to carry its load of chatterers, who are neither representative nor particularly helpful. There is always the possibility that one of these talks himself into humiliation when actuality catches up with fantasy, even in football.

Players of the calibre of Matthews, Finney, Lofthouse, are remembered as among the exemplary personalities of the game. In a modern setting they might very well not acquire the sheen that now goes with the personality label. Quiet, efficient, retiring men, they kept their eyes on the essentials. By their skills, of course, they gave pleasure to thousands, and more often than not in ordinary League fixtures. But they concentrated on doing and not on talking. They were private people in a way that seems no longer possible for a star. In the old days footballers made football. Nowadays it is too often the media which make both footballers and football.

*At the same time it must be remembered that the modern footballer is fitter than his predecessors. The average skill is on a higher level. This has the result of making the individual seem less individual, simply because collective organization counts for more. This, as a matter of fact, is in keeping with developments elsewhere. As society now is, what has to be done has to be done by groups rather than individuals. Hence the recent achievements of teams such as Leeds, Liverpool and Arsenal.*

But was it always so good in the old days? In 1950 the England team contained Alf Ramsey, Billy Wright, Tommy Finney, Wilf Mannion, and it lost in the World Cup to – the United States. It also lost to Spain although Matthews had been brought in. Matthews and Finney were wasted, one reads, because so far as the other English stars were concerned 'the genius had been stifled by years of stereotyped League service'. In 1953–4 England with Ramsey, Wright, Matthews, Mortensen, not only lost once to Hungary but twice, by 6–3 at Wembley (the first defeat of an English team at home), and 7–1 in Budapest. (But Hungary now has faded from the scene as one of the most prominent soccer nations.) With Matthews, Finney and Lofthouse in the 1954 World Cup England side disappointment came in the Quarter-Final when Uruguay won fairly easily. In 1958 England did not make the Quarter-Finals, but Wales did, and so did Northern Ireland!

No, the best was not always in the past! But the illusion that it was has a destructive influence on the game today. For a player it is not the last game but the next one that counts.

*Contrary to what everything else is saying, football on the field today is better organized, players are more dedicated; the modern player is aware of his role on the pitch, and to me the game now is far more exciting and enjoyable to play than when I started as a professional.*

# 7. The Present Structure of the Game

'*Who controls what, and why*'

The most worrying aspect of the present situation is the pressure applied to the professional player. As things are it is next to impossible to keep up a high and consistent standard across the whole year. Not that players don't try to do this. No more than professionals in other fields do they like to fall below their best, for 'job satisfaction' only exists when there is a feeling at least of reasonable competence. It is worth pointing out that, contrary to what some people might think, the footballer is not in the game only for the money.

The demands that are made do affect attitudes. In the old days – the 'good old days' – the annual work load consisted for the most part of the regular League fixtures. Nowadays the number of competitive matches in which a leading club is involved may touch seventy!

*If this is a matter of every other season then one can cope. Two seasons ago I did play over seventy games. I am quite sure if I had been subjected to these demands continually I would have been affected. Fortunately the next season my involvement was reduced to around fifty-odd. In that season the Wolves went to the semi-finals of both major Cups. To this day I don't know what is worse – the mental strain or the physical.*

*When the season starts the top clubs – such as Leeds, Liverpool, Arsenal and Tottenham – which also have to supply the bulk of players to the various national sides in Britain, are involved in intense competition right from the start. Taking into account that the League Cup and the European competitions start in September, and that the normal list of League fixtures has to be undertaken as well, twenty games or so will have been played by the end of October – that is, almost half of a total season's programme of only a few years ago.*

*For some teams the intensity of competitive football never lets up. Leeds and Liverpool have had eight years of involvement in European football. The prolonged physical and mental force that presses into the player, and into the team, is so great that in the end something has to give somewhere!*

*It hardly needs saying that if the pressures at the top are great, they are even greater at the bottom. A relegation haunted team may not have to play as many matches as one at the top, but each one is worth double the norm. Everyone has his sights on the wider European field. But relegation to the Second Division makes it look a very long way indeed. The sounds that come up from the doomed are pretty heart-rending.*

*There is no doubt that we have to do something to moderate the pressures. By making progress here we shall be doing something for the welfare of all the players concerned.*

*I was talking to Bill Shankly before our League match at Anfield in October 1973. He informed me that at that time his team was paying the penalty for the success of the 1972–3 season. They had won the Championship and the* EUFA *Cup. He reckoned the team suffered an anticlimax at the start of the new season. Everyone outside the Anfield camp thought they would start the season where they left off. It does not work out like that in football.*

*If you look back over the years you will find these trends and patterns exist. What has happened with Liverpool has been the reaction with most teams. An example of this in reverse is Leeds United. To all our surprise they lost to Sunderland in the 1973 Cup Final, lost the League title, and were beaten in the final of the European Cup-winners Cup (losing 0–1 to A.C. Milan at Salonika). During the close season everyone was writing them off, saying they were over the top, Billy Bremner was finished, and so was Johnny Giles, big Jack Charlton had retired, Don Revie was on his way to Everton. In short the rot had set in. At the time of writing they have just beaten Liverpool's post-war record of nineteen undefeated games, they have found a replacement for big Jack in Gordon McQueen, and Johnny Giles – except when out through injury – and Billy Bremner have never played better!*

*I am still waiting for retractions from the obituary writers! We still have not learned to accept these things that continue to happen in the greatest game in the world. In the case of Leeds all of this has been a good thing. I am sure everyone at Elland Road will learn a great deal from this whole experience.*

The secret of success is a combination of skill, fitness, will to win, and resources. Most of all resources. In brief the team that is going to succeed will have virtually two complete first class teams. That is to say, every position on the field will have a first choice man and a substitute who is fully equal to the demands put upon him by circumstances. In a hard and ruthless world there are no excuses for substitutes. So the pressure goes all the way down. Everyone agrees that the burden should be lighter, if for different reasons. We would begin by asking that this should be done for the benefit of the *average* player, who really carries the main weight of the responsibility. This is particularly the case within the structure of the English League.

It is interesting that the Chester Report made a proposal that is well worth considering, particularly since this came out of ideas that had previously been discussed by the League management committee. This committee, having considered changes in 'the pattern of football' has often found it difficult to secure a necessary three-quarters voting majority to implement them. Ten years ago the management committee thought about increasing the total of League clubs to 100, by adding eight to the existing ninety-two. This 100 would then be divided into five divisions, each of twenty. Between the top three divisions there would be a promotion–relegation exchange of four clubs, while each of the two lowest divisions would trade in two – as in the old days of Third Division South and North.

The Chester Committee looked at this, but determined that a First Division of twenty would be too much. For it is among the top teams here that fixture congestion is at its worst. The ideal number for a First Division, it is suggested, would be eighteen. The Chester Report is not dogmatic about numbers in the other divisions. It is considered important, however, that while the top three should be national in character, the lowest two should be regional. That is, Divisions 4 and 5 would be as the old Third Division North and South (with some Midland clubs necessarily changing from one to the other for the sake of accommodating the whole).

At once two proposals cry out for implementing. The First Division must certainly reduce. No other football country in the world runs a top division of twenty-two clubs, and in general elsewhere there is more regionalization on the next tier down. The position of practically every Third and Fourth Division club in England is now ludicrous. Gates do not even meet the travelling costs in many cases, and the greater the distance dividing clubs the less the interest as a rule. A team from Workington may go to Exeter to play. But how many supporters will accompany them? The writing is on the wall. But it is staggering how few there are who can read it.

In World Cup terms Third and Fourth Division clubs carry little weight. But in the context of English football they are not a negligible force. Nor should they be. As has already been stated, the standard is higher than it was. These clubs serve a community purpose, which in the future can very well be much more significant. Moreover without them the Pools would not be able to operate. The side in Division Three or Four keeps football of some quality alive in the neighbourhood. Local Derbys are the life-blood of this class of game, and with more regionalization there will be more in the way of local Derby interest. Over and above that are the bonuses that come from a modicum of success in FA or League Cup. What a great thing it is for a young player, for whom the Third or Fourth Division Club is a nursery, to get the taste of real combat in a cup-tie against a real top side.

If there are doubts about the projected Fourth and Fifth Divisions one only has to point out that there are already leagues operating perfectly satisfactorily on a regional basis. There is the Central League for the north, and the Football Combination for the south. These, of course, cater for Football League reserve teams. Otherwise there are the Southern League and the Northern Premier League – out of which came some of the newcomers to the Football League itself. Thus we see the pyramid structure, which is a useful structure in the main. But it does need urgent surgery at the points mentioned.

In England more, perhaps, than anywhere in the world the domestic structure is of the greatest importance. What we see at the very top of the pyramid is much affected by this fact. It is

F

also affected by the manner in which control is exercised. At the top of the pyramid, of course, is the national side. Or, one should say, the national sides. For what takes place within the pattern of English League football naturally has a profound, usually disastrous, influence on the other British national teams.

*If we stay with the English situation for the time being, I don't know what is going to happen over the next four or five years with the FA being the controlling body and the Football League organizing all the matches in the League programme. There is a conflict right from the start, because the Football League — as they have proved in the past — may not help Don Revie, as they did not help Ramsey, to plan the League so that nothing gets in the way of his full control over the national teams. The paradox was that when he was the League President Len Shipman was also an FA selector.*

*What one would like to see would be the Football League and the FA either redesigning the constitutional position so that they can work under one roof, or having one hat on so as to arrange for international matches to be played when there would be no other demands on players.*

*One might well look for a central controlling or co-ordinating body. This could be a delegate branch from the FA and the League with supervisory powers. Or it could be much stronger, a kind of overlord and watch-dog at the same time, with powers to step in at a moment's notice to deal with any problems that may arise. As it is the two bodies at present concerned leave themselves wide open for criticism in respect of international football. It has not proved possible to do the sensible thing, for instance, and cancel League matches prior to an International. Alternatively (but this is virtually impossible as things are) the FA should make its arrangements so as not to conflict with those of the League.*

*If both bodies were under one roof it would seem that the solution to many problems at domestic, national, and international level would be provided. When Poland and Italy played against England within a short time of each other at the end of 1973 their national bodies were more than content to forgo their respective League programmes where the result of this action was in the national interest.*

A good six months before the 1974 World Cup programme started the West German FA asked Borussia München Gladbach and FC Cologne to cancel all close season matches in order that their international players might be free. The Cologne manager Karl-Heinz Thielen spoke words that would be balm in an English team manager's ear: 'We'll do everything to help.' In eastern Europe the priorities are even more firmly established with regular attention to the national squad for months, let alone weeks, before an important competition.

*So far as Northern Ireland is concerned the selection of the team is only the first step in a sequence that is tragic or comic, depending on how you look at it. If the match is an away one we get together in London. But the unfortunate Irish FA Secretary has to spend all his time telephoning round for replacements for several of the original choices. For on the Saturday night immediately before any Irish FA match there is always a casualty list of chosen players who have been injured in League fixtures. The same goes for the Welsh team. When one's choice is limited to twenty players at the most, life can be very difficult indeed. Think of the effect on morale when key players have to withdraw through injury. But players should never be put in this position, virtually of choosing between club and country. It is most unfair on individuals. When it is the English team that is affected there is a lot of publicity. In the case of the smaller Associations there is less noise. Yet English League football owes a big debt to Wales and Ireland, not to mention Scotland, and the re-arrangement of League fixtures would be a nice* quid pro quo *so far as they are concerned and an enormous boon and blessing to the home side.*

*This brings us back to the idea of, say, eighteen teams in the First Division as recommended by Chester. I myself would prefer five divisions, each consisting of twenty teams. Although this only means a reduction of four League games in the First and Second Divisions, I am certain that these four games would reduce the fixture problems that successful sides encounter.*

*One should note here that in the Third and Fourth Divisions clubs take on forty-six League games without protest, and any other major involvement (in a Cup competition) is a most welcome bonus. The truth is, we are obliged to consider reorganizing the whole League structure for the few big guns. I am sure that, in spite of this, we should undertake the building of a new structure along the lines suggested for the sake of our national game.*

*It is not too far back since Chelsea were prevented from participating in the European Cup competition by the League. Now, however, the same League has its own Cup competition (which was not wished for by the big guns whose attitude was, it was not worth it) as a qualifier for entry into the UEFA competition. Here one may compare the Scottish attitude, for their clubs were in Europe before the English clubs.*

*If we were to reduce the fixture list in one of the ways suggested our administrators would be able to reorganize other competitions, particularly the League Cup. This could be put into a concentrated period, just as has been done in Scotland since the 1945–6 season. What excitement this would bring to the early part of the season. And by early November one club would already know that it had qualified for Europe.*

*Talking of the connection between England and Scotland, I am reminded of the Texaco Cup, which brings together sides from the two countries. This is a competition I am all in favour of keeping. It has produced some good football, and I know that Wolves have made a vast number of friends in Morton, Dundee, and Edinburgh because of this competition.*

*Having had a nightmarish experience when playing in the Anglo-Italian tournament in 1969–70, I would not participate in this competition again. It has clearly been shown that this tournament has won few admirers in England. In the opinion of a number of professional players it has been a more than painful experience. But the opinion of players in this, as in other respects, is not asked for.*

We see football as a kind of pyramid. From schoolboy football we go through Minor League, Sunday League, Regional League, English League with its strata of divisions, domestic Cup competitions, until we reach European football.

The pyramid goes higher and higher. For above the European competitions there is the World Cup. This hangs over the whole, sometimes in a malignant manner, for it tends to stultify progressive thinking. European football we understand and, on the whole, enjoy – even if there are reservations about some things that go on within the Italian concept of football. But these days, European football is also regional in that Europe itself is (certainly in American eyes) a region. Regionalization on the global scale becomes nonsensical. The zoning of national teams according to continent means that in the last stages of the World Cup there are inevitably some teams which are a good deal less competent than average. Indeed, one wonders how far some of the national teams from the Far East, from South America, from Africa, would go in infinitely less significant competitions. This is not a matter of keeping anyone out, but of wondering how, in the long run, justice is being served. With the best will in the world one is well aware that a Haitian or an Australian team will not draw the crowds. Yet it is a good thing for football that its influence should be so wide.

Time was when the Olympic Games would have taken a lot of the pressure off the World Cup. The football competition within the Olympic Games, we should remember, *was* a world-wide exercise, and until fairly recently it gave an opportunity to countries where football was important more as a recreation than as a spectacle. The collapse of Olympic Games football, through its being taken over by some of the top soccer nations, is a great pity. It is as though the Liverpools and Arsenals bulldozed a way into the FA Challenge Trophy Competition, which at present is dominated by the Staffords and Scarboroughs.

There are many political issues within the structure of football, and these become more obvious in the international than in the purely national sphere. Within FIFA there are a lot of knives flashing! It is felt by more than a few that England has at least four chances to qualify for every World Cup. It is thought that Wales, Scotland, and Northern Ireland (the position of Eire is rather obscure in all this) *are* in some way all part of England. That Wales, Scotland, and Northern Ireland are entitled to separate national identities is hard for some to accept. It must be confessed that it is sometimes hard even in England for this fact to be properly understood, so one should not take too much umbrage at the ignorance of those who are far away from the scene. But the fact remains that, so far as we are concerned, Wales, Scotland and Northern (and Southern) Ireland are separate footballing nations because of their different traditions and histories.

A national Great Britain team looks a good prospect on paper. It may even be pointed out that it used to be a Great

Britain team that took part in the Olympic Games. It is, of course, easier to come to suitable arrangements in such a matter where amateurs rather than professionals are involved. There are fewer vested interests to stand in the way. Yet even here there were difficulties, so that one could not envisage arriving at a fully united Great Britain side unless supernatural forces were to lend some aid. In any case political considerations do allow for two Koreas and two Germanys and two Irish teams – to take only the most obvious examples – in World Cup football. If all the British sides are to be reduced to one, then there will need to be a good deal of consolidation elsewhere. Nonetheless the battle concerning British interests will continue for a long time, simply because it is frequently felt that British football administrators justify themselves merely by recourse to history – by saying, this is as it was, so this is as it must remain! Which brings us back to FA and Football League. We can cope with situations on the world stage when we have a more unified control at home.

*The more one looks into these matters, the more one realizes that we in England are too much bound by the past. The Chester Report suggests overhauling the constitution of the FA so that professional players can add their experience and directly influence decision-making. This is common sense; but common sense does not always prevail.*

*There have been many changes in the structure of the game over the last decade concerning the interests, welfare and livelihood of the players. The players are always the last to hear of them!*

# 8. Learning to be a Professional

*'What it's all about'*

Football is a profession in which an early start is desirable. It is not the only one. One knows, for instance, that great musical artists have often been trained from childhood. Musical performance and football have this in common, that they depend on finely controlled physical movements which must become instinctive. One might use the word 'automatic' except that this tends to assume that the human being is a machine. Some people may very well think that some performers are little more, but they are wrong. For only when one has that quickness of response that is termed automatic is one able to show individuality, originality, creativeness, or whatever the quality is that makes the working life of artist or footballer worthwhile.

The beginnings of careers that rely on physical responsiveness are always tricky. Naturally, one supposes in the first place that there is an early talent to be developed. But it is frequently difficult to determine whether what one takes to be talent really is such – and supposing it is – whether it will prove sufficiently durable to stand up to hard reality.

Up to a point it is possible to achieve some measure of success in a particular craft with any reasonably healthy material in which there is an initial willingness to undertake training. If one starts a child of six on the piano or the violin, and if he has a 'musical ear' and is prepared to do a daily stint of practice under expert guidance, he may turn out to be reasonably competent. But whether he will be a great virtuoso is something that lies in the lap of the gods. So it is with football. In trying to produce a genius by conscious endeavour one too often succeeds merely in putting yet another psychological misfit into a world unkind to psychological misfits. Too early specialization means that only one set of abilities is developed. It is bad enough when the over-specialized Doctor of Philosophy finds himself on the market, but his specialized training has only been undertaken after his most impressionable years. His general education has been previously fairly wide-ranging. There have been cases of young musicians whose sole aim had been music almost from infancy. Of these at least some (and not the least famous) found life more than difficult, because they had not been fitted for its many phases in any proper manner.

So far as football is concerned, we may start with the premise that almost every healthy, sport-loving lad in Britain thinks – with varying degree of intensity – that he would like one day to play for Arsenal, Spurs, Newcastle, Manchester United . . . Keenness is a fine attribute. It is a first duty to make sure that a boy's keenness endures. To become really expert at anything requires patience as well. It is only too true that perfection comes after much practice – if indeed it comes even then. In the early stages emphasis is on practice. But to go on with the exercises that make up the early part of a career needs a sense of purpose, and the continuing support and help of people of more experience. There is an awful lot of hard graft.

Because football has become a matter of national prestige the search for talent starts early in every country where football is played seriously. And at a very early stage, where promise is detected, some expert coaching is made available. In the eastern European countries – where vast sums of money are invested by every government in physical education – such coaching is undertaken within the educational system. Just how effective this is is shown in athletics and in swimming. Football is a team activity and, while one may teach the individual to make the best use of his individual talents, it is hard to know what techniques produce that intangible essence which we call team spirit. However, those who are well acquainted with Russian, Polish, Yugoslav, Czech, Hungarian, Bulgarian, or East German football will realize that technical excellence is not to be underrated! Nor, as shown in the 1974 World Cup, does its possession hinder development of a corporate sense of purpose.

At the same time awareness of team cohesion begins earlier in Britain than elsewhere. It is not long before the primary schoolboy discovers that he is required for some sort of football team. How long depends to some extent on locality. The small boy in Manchester, or Wolverhampton, or Liverpool, thinks he knows what is expected from him. By the time he is in the last year of the primary school a boy who has made the school team has already taken the first steps towards a career in football – even if he himself does not know it. In the secondary school life in football seems to begin in earnest. For some it may be said that life begins in earnest.

*In many areas there are teachers with special qualifications. Some have taken specialized courses in Colleges of Education (some colleges of course are well known for their expertise in physical training), and some have taken courses in coaching organized by the FA. One finds a lot of young teachers these days who are sitting for their FA Preliminary Badges. Those who are successful at the first stage often go on to complete the course for the full Badge.*

*When a boy of, say, twelve years of age seems to show promise, the word gets round. If it gets far enough round the school team may find itself attracting unfamiliar spectators, with a special interest in the proceedings. A scout passes information back to headquarters, and when the information sounds encouraging a senior scout decides discreetly to have a look at the situation. The really promising boy (unknown to him) goes onto a card for the records of the big club. The tabs are kept on him – sometimes, of course, by more than one big club. At a suitable point in time suggestions are made that the young teenager shall ally himself with a professional club.*

*It is fine that boys shall be encouraged, and for a boy to be called to a famous ground for coaching is very thrilling. But here it should be noted that the process is one that is characterized by hit and miss. An awful lot of young footballers of talent are certainly missed at the first stage – though some of them surface later on.*

The FA is quite clear as to what is allowed and what is not. A boy of fourteen may be registered by a club as an 'Associated Schoolboy'. This gives him the chance of receiving special tuition in football, perhaps two evenings a week in term time, and in the daytime during school holidays. The 'Associated Schoolboy' may not play for the club to which he is attached until he has reached the statutory school-leaving age. This, of course, is now sixteen. While he is still at school and above the statutory leaving age a boy is expected to put his loyalty at the disposal of his school team (presuming he belongs to it) in the first place. The FA expresses the hope, however, that in the case of boys who are not selected for school teams their headmasters will not place any obstacle in the way of their playing for other teams organized by outside bodies.

The 'Associated Schoolboy' is registered with a club belonging to the Football League (and to some other clubs which have a minimum of twelve full-time professionals) by a form of 'Attachment'. This is signed by the boy, his parent (or guardian), his headteacher, and duly witnessed. And all this process is in accordance with the determinations of the FA and English Schools FA, and the representative teacher organization.

A boy who has the status of 'Associated' may very well find out in due course that he has tied himself to one club. In the first place he felt flattered, no doubt. And his family probably felt flattered too.

Some parents want to get in on the act and to profit at the expense of their offspring. In case this sounds too censorious of one sort of parents who suspect that they have produced talent out of the ordinary, it should be said that all parents tend to think themselves the originators of genius unless the evidence to the contrary is absolutely overwhelming. The practice of exploiting talented youngsters is not limited to football, and is to be deplored wherever it occurs. While some parents of schoolboy footballers see possibilities for themselves in the interest shown in their sons by big clubs others take the longer view. It is not unknown for parents to ask for a letter from a club promising that their sons should at the proper time be taken on as apprentices. Equally it is not unknown for clubs to give such promises.

On the other hand there are many who are unused either to contracts or to the ways of the world. There is a great moral responsibility on the clubs and, indeed, on everybody else connected with promoting the idea of football as a career to susceptible schoolboys. It is clear that there is a less than attractive face to football organization when it comes to the hunt for talent. For real talent, in whatever field, is always in short supply.

One would certainly wish to put in a warning note here. A schoolboy invited to attend for coaching at a famous club should not think that this is the end of the beginning, that from this point on there are no impediments to the acquiring of fame and fortune. There can be nasty disillusionments, and a wise parent will make sure that his football keen son will at the same time benefit to the full from educational opportunities. It is too often assumed that boys of athletic talent are merely liabilities in the wider sphere of education. The assumption is a frequent cause of later disaster.

There is a curious and alarming phrase embedded in (of all places) the Regulations of FIFA. No doubt to many the terms in which regulations, rules, bye-laws, hire purchase agreements, contracts, and so on, are expressed are boring. Alas, the more boring such things seem, the more carefully they should be studied!

*The phrase which caught my eye was in Article 14, about 'Professional Players' and the conditions of their transfer. WHEN THE PLAYER HAS REGAINED HIS FREEDOM a certificate of transfer etc. may be asked for. The language means what it says. But where else at this stage in time is 'regaining freedom' talked about, except as regards prisoners. It reminds one of the southern States in America before the Civil War.*

Some plain speaking is called for in the matter of 'Associated Schoolboys'. For there is no doubt that there are too many blind eyes being turned on too many abuses and malpractices. In a memorandum about 'Schoolboys and School games' the FA says that 'one of the important aspects of games in school is the opportunity of developing a boy's sense of loyalty and honour'. Again, the words sound fine, although they may seem to echo some of the wordy ideas about loyalty and honour that were in the air when the FA was founded. But they are some way off target in the modern setting. Loyalty, in this context, boils down to this: that what a boy wants to do of his own volition in his own free time (Saturday is stated) depends on what his headmaster thinks he ought to be doing. If a boy wants to play football for his school team he will play for it the better if he is not nagged about 'loyalty'. If a boy is a naturally good player and if his school team is a bad one, no one gains anything if he is prevented from playing elsewhere in a setting where he can gain experience and greater pleasure. If a pupil owes loyalty to a school, the school owes a greater loyalty to the pupil. Fortunately this kind of unwritten contract does not go unregarded. There are some excellent football teams in schools of all sorts, and most boys still take pride in being picked.

The 'Associated Schoolboy' scheme started ten years ago, in large measure to prevent the kind of slave-market transactions that took place whenever an important English Schools' FA match took place. The avowed aim of the scheme was to provide 'training and coaching' – fine. But what happens to a boy who is signed for a club whose ground is a hundred miles from where he lives? To this question, one must confess that there sometimes must be a cynical reply. The causes for the question arising and the consequences that flow from it need looking at.

*I can only speak here directly of our club in this respect. Schoolboys who live in other towns and who have signed blue forms are invited to Molineux, when the club considers they merit it, for a trial period that can last a few days or even up to the length of the school holidays. Any boy who is invited is put into approved digs and every day after morning training he is taken to the Molineux Hotel (which the club owns) for a good lunch. This applies also to boys who may have left school but who are not yet at the apprentice stage.*

The Chester Report made it quite clear that in its opinion material considerations too often surround the scheme for schoolboys. It stated quite bluntly that, 'the financial stakes involved can impair the judgement of parents and schoolmasters and lower the ethical standards of League Clubs'. This buying and selling of children – for that is what it is – is incredible. More incredible is the fact that authorities connive at it – and still speak of 'loyalty and honour'.

*This is not the end of this matter, by any means. Let us suppose that a boy has signed on as an 'Associated Schoolboy' at the age of fourteen. For him this is wonderful. He goes to the ground of his favourite club (or the one that has become his favourite club for reasons that are not all that clear to him), and while he does not strike up immediate friendship with the famous players of the club staff, whose pictures are on his bedroom wall, he can at least sometimes see them on their way to their training. That is likely to be in the holidays, for in term time schoolboy training is at night, in the gymnasium or on the practice ground by flood-light. The average boy is less interested in training than in getting involved in five-a-side football or in a normal practice game. But under the coach (the schoolboy at this point is a long way outside the knowledge of the manager of the club) the boy learns first certain basic requirements, such as kicking (not as easy as it looks!), trapping, heading, and so on, and to correct what appear to be his weaknesses. This, at any rate, is what should be done if not always what actually is done. Competition in a team comes later.*

*Some boys drop out. They get caught up with pop groups, with other sports, or they become bored. The Saturday glamour is curiously absent from the stadium on weekdays when the terraces are empty and there are only to be heard demanding voices of the coach and the trainer. Fame and fortune look far off.*

*But the dedicated boy sticks it out. Although he is a schoolboy it is likely that his mind is made up. Professional football, that is the life for him, and his dreams, encouraged often by those who should know better, lead him to neglect most other things. What practically everybody has missed up to this point is that the boy's options are very limited. He has already lost a large part of his freedom.*

When an 'Associated Schoolboy' leaves school his registration (with the FA) may not be transferred to another club without the consent of the club that signed him as a schoolboy in the first place. If he wishes to become an apprentice professional he must become registered as such with the club to which he is already attached. The holding club, it is true, is required to decide whether to take him on as an apprentice within a 'reasonable time' (six months?). If there is the slightest chance of his proving any sort of asset he will, of course, be taken on. This may be what he wants. On the other hand, it may not be what he wants, nor what is in his best interest. That does not count. What does count is the blue form he signed at the age of fourteen, hardly knowing anything of its implications. The FA is not only aware of this but condones it. Loyalty? Honour?

The Chester Report recommended that the Associated Schoolboy Scheme (also in Wales and Scotland) should be altered so that a boy could be free to make his own choice of club at the end of the period of schoolboy status. The one mark of consideration for the club is that no approaches should be made to a schoolboy on the books within the last three months of his activity in that status without the club's permission. It has already been pointed out that nothing at all has come out of the Chester Report up to date, except for the overhauling of disciplinary procedures.

*A number of clubs, I am afraid, have a very selfish attitude. I do remember, however, what happened to one friend of mine. Sammy Chapman, who showed so much promise when we both lived in Belfast in the early fifties, was taken to Manchester, where he went to school for a bit. I think this kind of thing can have a great effect. It was obvious that Sammy was looked after very well with Manchester United and his welfare was well taken care of. But that kind of thing remains uncommon.*

*What I would like to see in every town and city is a centre where budding young footballers of school age can have tuition, coaching, and instruction from professional players. Obviously this would be a considerable expense – probably to the ratepayer and the taxpayer – but I think we would be providing a really valuable facility. Over the years we have seen how many boys who eventually became household names slipped through the net and never had the opportunity (say at Wolves) but went up and down the country to get an opportunity elsewhere. If we had a centre I would be ready to help and certainly many of my professional colleagues would gladly devote time to the encouragement of the stars of tomorrow.*

This brings us back to the necessity for the professional football club fitting into the community and, indeed, fulfilling some of the purposes for which it was formed into a Company. There is no doubt that a soccer centre – or whatever it might be called – would be feasible. It would in the end be of all-round benefit, to those who wanted to make football a worthwhile hobby as well as to those who aimed at it as a profession. The 'Associated Schoolboy' label, and the scheme as it now stands, would be rendered superfluous. And the boys whose interests are our concern would have freedom *and* opportunity. One present difficulty – although not, one would think, a major one – is that, however good a professional footballer is, he is not acceptable as a coach without proper official creditation.

Before 1964 a boy who wanted to try his luck at professional football tried to get taken on as a ground-staff boy. As such he did a lot of odd jobs and could be got rid of with the greatest of ease after three or, if he was luckier, six months. What happens now is rather different when a boy has an 'Associated' label to cash in for the prospect of apprenticeship.

The situation may be affected by any understanding arrived at by parents as mentioned on p. 90, but this is unofficial. On the official level we now have to take account of the 1973 raising of the school leaving age. Prior to this a boy could register as an apprentice between his fifteenth and seventeenth birthday with both the FA and the League for a period to end on his eighteenth birthday. The form signed by the boy commits him to observe the rules, regulations, and bye-laws of the FA and the club. Here one can only hope that these rules and regulations are read by every boy – and his parent or guardian who is required to be a consenting party – beforehand. If this were always done it would eliminate a good deal of later misunderstanding and unhappiness. Signing any contract means giving up some freedom of action; it is as well to ensure that the offering is not absolute. Before any parent or guardian commits a boy to accepting and signing either an apprentice's or a professional's form it is wise to seek the advice of the PFA.

Apprenticeship ends when the boy is eighteen. Then he must decide if he wishes to become a professional, or to revert to amateur status – a possibility envisaged within the apprentice form of contract. So far as the club involved is concerned, however, it will generally have made up its mind by the time the boy is seventeen. At that age a boy is entitled to become a full-time professional. Should a club have any doubts about the potential of an apprentice there is, of course, an advantage in having a year's grace. In general, for reasons stated, the boy will have made up his mind long before, and will probably have closed the avenues that might have been open to him outside of football. If this is the case it is not because of any failing on the part of the PFA who have an Education Officer whose purpose is to see that boys are not denied knowledge of and help towards continuing education. The importance of this is only too obvious in a profession not notable for security.

It may be argued that being an apprentice footballer is in itself highly educational, in a broad sense, and entirely worthwhile. What does the apprentice do?

*Normally the apprentices arrive at the ground at nine o'clock. Most of them know what they have to do. They lay out the training kit of the first and second teams. They look after the boots of all the pros, changing the studs, cleaning them, seeing that they are dried. Under supervision they clean the bathrooms, wash the toilets, sweep the place up generally, and polish any brass doorknobs there may be. Sometimes they wash the manager's car, and the trainer's, and even the secretary's . . . Most of these menial jobs are not relished and are done with a good deal of resentment. I have often said during my time with six clubs that in many ways this is nothing but cheap labour, with nothing to do with being an apprentice footballer.*

*It may, then, seem strange that the Chairman of the PFA should tolerate the conditions that are facing most apprentices. It should of course be said that there are ninety-two League clubs and the conditions do vary. Some clubs treat their apprentices well and some treat them badly. But when we look in at a First Division club we find about fourteen young boys. When they are not doing what I have already described they are painting the ground, the goalposts, cutting the grass, and − at the end of the season − helping to re-lay and re-seed the pitch. Our predicament, and the reason why one has to seem to tolerate the situation at the moment, is that if the PFA were to step in to tell clubs they should employ their apprentices in a role more befitting their future status the clubs would cut down the number of apprentices.*

*When a boy is about to sign for a club his father and his mother (or one of them, or a guardian) are brought down to the area (if it is a club in another town other than their own) and shown around. They can* see what the boy is coming to and the accommodation in which he will live. Once the form is signed, or after a professional form is signed in the case of a boy who comes in direct at that stage, all the little privileges cease. Like all the rest of us he has to learn to fend for himself in the game.

There is a degree of segregation within a club. The boys have all their chores done and the professionals have arrived by ten o'clock. The first team squad stay together. The reserve team stay with the reserve team trainer. The apprentices stay with the youth team coach and are trained on their own. Two or three of the boys may come along with the first team. Not to take any part in the training session, but to fetch the ball back when it goes behind the goal.

It is like taking a dog for a walk. Every now and then you throw a stick and he obediently chases after it to bring it back to you. If you question this with a trainer or a coach the answer is that it is all part of the job. I disagree. Knowing what I now know I don't think I could ever have disciplined myself to the mundane, repetitive jobs that go along with being an apprentice. I have always felt that if I were an apprentice as things are today I would point out that I was an apprentice footballer, not an apprentice odd-job man!

Things have improved in that most clubs employ an old professional who has come to the end of his career to look after the lads and to supervise them in their training. But after they have done their menial jobs. About training, I would like to say that most of the young boys are trained too much and that, at this stage, not enough emphasis is put on control and skill.

Training for the apprentices stops at half-past twelve, or when whoever is in charge says so. They are back in the afternoon as a rule to tidy up, or to clean out the dressing rooms. After that what they do is at the discretion of the trainers.

The routine is more or less the same every day of the week, though it may vary a little if there is a mid-week game. The Saturday results have a major bearing on the next week's routine. If the first team does well then the head trainer can be in a very generous mood.

Some clubs give the apprentices an odd afternoon off. Others expect them to report regularly, to stop them from hanging around town and the coffee bars. Friday in any case is a short day, but the apprentice can expect to find himself back at the ground in the afternoon to help the trainer put the skips together, that is, if the team is playing away from

G

*home. The apprentice may report on Saturday morning to give a hand to the trainer to lay out the kit for the afternoon game. At this the apprentice feels himself to be honoured and this simple task can be the highlight of the week. Some apprentices will turn up on Sunday morning – to clean the baths, which have been used the day before.*

*Such is the week of the apprentice footballer. If he were paid for what he did by the hour he would receive a lot more than the £8 or so he actually gets.*

Apart from the pay the apprentice footballer does exactly the demanding tasks that used to be (and sometimes still are) carried out for big boys by little boys in public schools. In this connection they used to speak of discipline and obedience. But the practices were progressively discontinued by the enlightened. After all, big boys could just as well clean their own shoes.

*Many apprentices live away from home. Here we meet another hazard that has to be faced. Boys arrive into the busy life of a famous club often from distant places in Scotland, or Wales, or from across the water. And they feel homesick. Sometimes this feeling is acute, even unbearable. It is well known that when he came to Manchester from Belfast, George Best had this feeling to an overpowering degree – and he went home. Billy Bremner suffered similarly when he first arrived in Leeds. I can understand all of this, for I too found it hard to settle down in a strange place, where people spoke in a strange way, and where the habits and customs were alien to all that I had known. This was in Portsmouth. But I was lucky to make friends there who helped me to acclimatize, and I soon felt much better after my first couple of matches in the first team. However, for the young – and not always the young – player there is frequently a sense of loneliness – the loneliness, one may say, of the long distance footballer.*

*Boys coming from far away have to have somewhere to live. A number of clubs, to their credit, have established hostels for the youngsters on their staffs. Otherwise digs are found by the chief scout of a club. In many ways boys living in lodgings are better off than local lads. For years boys living at home with their parents have been penalized because football clubs don't consider them as needing support in respect of maintenance. This is obviously a time when boys need all the good food they can get. Yet I have known cases where the parents of a boy attached to a club but living at home have found it a great struggle to make ends meet.*

*I have referred previously to the importance of schooling. It is disturbing when one finds promising lads in every way who have been so much enthralled by their surroundings in football that every idea of schooling is thrown aside.*

*But why worry? Everything is organized for the present or the former apprentice, and he does not need to think for himself. Right from the start a professional footballer is told what to do. His strip is washed for him. His boots are cleaned for him. Whenever he travels the travelling arrangements are made for him. The little world in which he is brought up, as 'Associate Schoolboy', as apprentice, as professional, is unbelievably ordered. The founders of the FA, just over a hundred years ago, considered that football was a necessary part of a proper apprenticeship to leadership. It cannot be said that this principle is cited at the present time by those who determine the lives of the young aspirants to football fame. Theirs is to do, not to reason why!*

The statistics of success and failure in football apprenticeship are alarming. In 1966 of the apprentices taken on by League clubs about 65 per cent were able to continue into the profession. That sounds not too bad, but if the same figures were produced in an academic context, after the youngsters concerned had been carefully selected, they would sound not too good. However, if sixty-five out of every hundred apprentices were able to go on as full-time professionals there would be few grounds for real complaint, provided that the ones who left the game at the end of their apprenticeship had something worthwhile to turn to. More often than not they don't.

Four years later, that is in 1970, the figures were infinitely worse. The successes now numbered only 38 per cent. It is suspected that now, in 1974, the figures are still more discouraging. The Burnley Chairman, Bob Lord, says that so far as his club is concerned if two youngsters a year are developed into first class players that is good. 'If you do that,' he is quoted, 'you've got a very successful youth policy. In fact, you're nearly on the doorstep of Utopia.'

To be fair Burnley, like West Ham, Stoke City, Wolves, and a few other clubs, superintend training carefully and every attempt is made to enable those who don't make the grade as footballers to find a congenial setting and occupation elsewhere.

It cannot, however, be sufficiently emphasized that there is much that remains to be put right in respect of the early stages of a football career. There is:

An undercover battle for oustanding young players going on between clubs and unscrupulous parents expressing more concern for money than the welfare of their sons. Outstanding talent, even in its embryo form, commands a high price and it's not surprising. A former schoolboy international bought for £3000 has been sold for £100 000 and, at this moment, there is another schoolboy on offer to anybody who 'will put £5000 on the kitchen table'.

So wrote Franklyn Wood in *The Sunday Times* at the beginning of the 1973–4 season, and then went on to expose one particular case of exploitation.

Those ultimately responsible for this kind of situation are difficult to find, and if found will evade their share of criticism, by looking elsewhere. In the end, however, we are all responsible up to a point. Football is a national game and a popular game. It is then also a national and a popular responsibility. That means you and us, and them!

*I don't wish to disillusion a would-be Bobby Charlton, only to show him what is in store.*

# 9. Independence and Insecurity

*'We are still waiting for a fair deal for all'*

There is no doubt that football in the end is the classic province where only the fittest can survive. The upbringing of a young player is strict, but it also confers some privileges. Early on, when accepted into the first team or even the reserve squad, there is a lot of money to be had. A lot, that is, compared with what a youngster earns outside the game, or what is given to a student of the same age group. This, however, should be set against the insecurities that afflict the player during his career, the possibility of serious injury (even though insurance provides some fall-back), of lost form, of being put onto the transfer market and from here moving down. (The majority of transfers in fact are from higher to lower divisions – but these are not usually those that hit the headlines.) Throughout his career there is a considerable restriction of personal freedom. That has already been shown.

There is no doubt that many people applaud the very thing that should be deplored – the restricting of freedom of individuals, supposedly in their own interests. The youngster learns 'discipline' – a word thrown at footballers with sickening frequency – by having his every action dictated for him. He learns loyalty. Efficiency results from the process of rigorous training. But at the same time (this will be taken up in the next chapter) footballers are also written off as unruly, undisciplined, brutal – the choice is yours without paying any money.

The unthinking part of the public and of the media want to have their cake and eat it. Discipline is said to be good for the young professional. The established professional, however, is often depicted as entirely lawless. Truth, of course, has many sides. But in seeking it one should look for more than one side.

Some youngsters do survive the rigours of their training and emerge with credit. Some don't turn out well.

Having said that, we have done no more than describe what happens to boys, usually from a different background, who have been sent away to boarding school. This type of training is also applauded by those whose distance from it lends enchantment.

When the young footballer has become established (that is perhaps too strong a word to apply to a profession of such uncertainty, but let it pass) he goes into a higher income bracket. But what he earns is to be set against the continuing prohibitions which are placed round him. Many if not most of these would not be tolerated in any other occupation.

The rules which determine the way of life of a footballer are arbitrarily contrived by the FA, the Football League, and each club. These rules are made up without reference to the players, supposedly in the interests of the game. It is only simple justice that in any reasonable society those who are obliged to live according to certain rules, and to observe certain restrictions of their liberty, should be there, or at least adequately represented, when the rules are drawn up. The very idea would give the general run of football administration a blue fit, which only goes to show how strong is the principle of paternalism. The concept of the professional footballer as one who is incapable of thinking except through his feet is one of the insults that fly about so often without challenge that it is taken by people outside of football (whose own thinking processes can seem pretty inefficient!) as true.

To be fair the notion that sportsmen are stupid is one that is rife in respect of other kinds of sportsmen than soccer professionals. The Oxford–Cambridge rugby match is no longer what it once was, because the teams are supposedly less good than, say, before the war. More than one famous old Blue has complained of the present insistence on students earning their university places on academic merit. In their day it was different. A good reputation as a front row forward or a three-quarter was what counted with the admission tutors. Intellect was even a positive disadvantage. If one reads of American universities, even in serious journals, one learns that very few of their football scholars (looked after even more carefully than English League footballers) are more than just literate. The whole business of the link between stupidity and sporting excellence has been cooked up by commercial interests, who would be (and are) aghast were sportsmen actually to answer back – if given the chance.

We could find countless examples in the journalism of football to bear out this contention. One will suffice. Here we find someone who repeats the general impression, but has the grace to wish that things could be otherwise! Frank McGhee, of the *Daily Mirror*, recently condemned the system under which footballers live because it fails to allow them to develop their personalities,

... Not only as performers, but, more important, as men.

Today's players are cosseted, protected, sheltered, led by the hand and hidden. They are also reprimanded, fined and sometimes suspended for stepping out of line.

The result is that so many players not only can't talk or won't talk. Too many don't have anything significant to say if they do talk – with the permission of their manager . . .

The manager is often a restrictive force, because he too is restricted. His situation is summed up in simple terms in an article in the *West Indian World*:

The vast majority of club bosses are retired players who usually left school at an early age. Football and ultimately Managership is more the Holy Grail of ambition for the working-class lads all over the world.

If they make the grade at thirty-five they can be earning up to £30 000 a year as managers with sometimes the power to spend a million a year on new players.

But to most dilettantes who really run football, managers remain as grown-up working-class lads who are always dispensable.

So we see how all the professionals of the game are in it together – but split into two factions, each suspicious of the other and in doubt as to what may happen up above at Board level.

*If this sounds gloomy it is fair to say that in my own experience the relationship between directors, administrators, and players has in some respects improved over the last few years. At my previous clubs the conversations I had with directors did not last more than a few seconds. In fact dialogue was based on 'Good morning', 'Good afternoon', 'Goodbye', 'Are we going to win today?', 'I think we may get a point at, say, Anfield'. It is only fair to say that I do get on very well with the directors at Molineux, and am on a good relationship with the entire board. Also I couldn't meet a nicer man than our Chairman, John Ireland.*

*With the administrators, however, one still feels that we, the players, are looked down on. It's always them and us. The situation has changed somewhat since the abolition of the maximum wage in 1961. Since that time new ideas on justice within the game have at least been brought forward. In 1966 there was an investigation into the football industry by Political and Economic Planning (or PEP), which recommended freedom of control, After that, two years later, came the Chester Report. This, like the earlier report, was concerned with 'the means by which the game may be developed for the public good'.*

*As in other branches of industry and of entertainment the body that represents the workers – in this case the players – must bear a great deal of responsibility. For obvious reasons the PFA has a limited membership – of about 2500 members – and, in contrast to many other bodies, has only limited bargaining power. Throughout the years the PFA has acted with great responsibility, and (as is shown in earlier chapters) has achieved a great deal. In recent times it could have achieved more had the Football League, for instance, shown itself more prepared to meet the PFA at least half-way over certain issues. One recalls the extension of the playing season and the introduction of sponsored competitions, for example, without prior consultation.*

*One is frequently told that one should not look back to the 'bad old days'. Not only in football. But sometimes one fears that they may come again. Ever since the inception of football the players have been misused by all and sundry. Football clubs have bought and sold them in the same way as livestock, and with no more rights in some instances. The absurdities of the present transfer system are acknowledged by all those who have the real interests of the game at heart.*

'At the current rate,' said Cliff Lloyd after attending a meet-

Minutes of Meeting held at
the Imperial Hotel Manchester
Dec 2.07

Proposed by W. Bull
Seconded by C. Roberts and
carried.
That Mr. Meredith take the chair
Mr. Meredith then read the list
of clubs present and the replies
he had received to the circulars
sent out.
Proposed by Mr. McCombie
Seconded by Mr. Turnbull & carried
That Mr. C. R. L. Menzies be Secretary
pro tem.
Proposed by C. Roberts— That each
club have a representative—withdrawn
Proposed by B. Lipsham
Seconded by. H. C. Broomfield
& carried. that 5 sections be
formed. North. Lancashire &
Yorkshire. Midlands. London &
South. and West.

First page of first Minute Book of Players' Union, 2 December
1907, with W. Meredith as Chairman

Top left: Rough play in 1893, R. Kelso (Everton) up-ended
Top right: Cover of *Football Players Magazine*, September 1913
Above: Rough play in 1827, engraving by Robert Cruikshank

Below: Jimmy Howcroft, a classical referee

Bottom: Final word; from William Pickford's book of cuttings, 1907

### THE VISIT OF ENGLAND'S GREATEST REFEREE.

**MR. J. HOWCROFT.**

We do not overstate our case when we refer to the Subject of our sketch as "England's Greatest Referee." Jimmy Howcroft, or to give him his full title Mr. J. T. Howcroft started "tootling the whistle" 28 years ago and has been on the League List 27 consecutive years. He has officiated at every big "Derby Day" in England, also on every ground in the old Southern League, First League, and Second League. To give our readers just a rough idea of the trust reposed in "Jimmy" by the "powers that be" he has refereed *26 Internationals*, and in every continental country with the exception of Russia; 3 English Cup *semi-finals* and *one final 1920*. Mr. Howcroft has refereed more Cup Ties and League matches where the crowd have broken in owing to overcrowding than any other "Ref" in England for 14 years.

Jimmy was contemporary with such giants as Mr. "Jack" Lewis, Mr. "Jimmy" Mason, Mr. Taylor, etc., etc. These "giants" of the past would be the first to admit to-day that for sheer ability, coolness, and personality the "gentleman from Bolton" holds first place.

To convey to our readers the power Mr. Howcroft wields over players even in their "excited moments." Imagine Season 1922-3. Two First League contestants one side the Spurs, Banks the old outside right careering along with the ball. Full back of the opposside fouls Banks rather badly. He comes to earth rather heavily, up he jumps arm raised to strike the delinquent. Just at that moment a whistle blows, and Master Banks very much like a school-boy before the master remember that football's the game, not fisticuffs. For 14 years Jimmy travelled to Scotland and Ireland without a break, but to-day he cannot spare the time. We do not think anyone enjoys the work more than he, and we can assure our readers to see him in action is "real joy."

Mr. Howcroft holds the record for League Service 28 years.—the next nearest having 16 years to his credit.

Usually the crowd pay their token of respect to this "great official" by giving him a heartier cheer than they usually extend to their own team.

This is the first occasion Mr. Howcroft has visited the town of Crewe and we hope our supporters will pay him that tribute he so justly deserves, let us prove to him that though we are bottom club we still retain the true characteristics of good sportsmanship.

Drama at night; a full house at Molineux

ing of the International Professional Footballers' Federation at the end of 1973, 'a player will cost half-a-million in England before long, and who can afford that?'

*When we were considering this section of the book, the CIR Report in connection with the position of footballers under the Industrial Relations Act had not appeared. When it was published it endorsed much of our thinking. As for the Chester Report this was overtaken by the Act and by entry into the Common Market.*

*The French have had freedom of contract for two years, the Dutch got it not long ago, and the Germans will have it too before long. It's only a matter of time before we have it in Britain.*

*Freedom of contract is basic to the future prosperity of the game. A big step was taken in 1963 when Mr. Justice Wilberforce gave a judgement in favour of George Eastham and against Newcastle United, because the practices then applying so far as retention and transfer of players were concerned were 'in unreasonable restraint of trade'. The Eastham case is not only a landmark in English case-history, but it has served as a precedent in similar cases on the continent. The fight for freedom does not only have to be fought in 'England's green and pleasant land'.*

It has been said often enough that we are in Europe, but very few really seem to believe this. Or if they do, have no intention to see how we are and how we may be affected. Of course, there is European football, and we feel that we belong to that. Not only that, but the average fan – and many others besides – would like us to run the whole show. Whatever else is uncertain, this fact is certain: we will *not* run European football. What the end result of the Treaty of Rome will be in respect of the football profession will take a long time to determine. But it is likely that players will get together, as members of other professions do, to protect their interests.

We may have grounds for complaining about the place in society occupied by a professional footballer in England. But we have had far better relationships with employers than has been the case in some countries. Notably in France.

In 1972 the National Union of Professional Footballers in France called a strike. They had many reasons for complaint.

Being French they placed first the threat to freedom represented not only by contracts but also by the behaviour of those who operate in the background of the game. In a document defining the policy and ideals of the profession M. Jacques Bertrand, Secretary of the National Union, described these as 'tricksters' and demanded their total exclusion from football. He urged that directors and players should be aware 'that to conclude a Professional Footballer's Contract is to effect an important, serious and grave act'.

The National Union drafted a charter for the career footballer. 'But', wrote Bertrand, 'it unfortunately seems that Management is more pre-occupied with the negotiation of Contracts to convert into investments than with the concern of setting up a new Rules for a profession which might attract exceptional players through causing them to benefit from their merit.' This statement was followed by another which we believe should be the answer to those who ask here and now in what way our own football can be improved:

It is through the players and the conditions which they receive that football will be revitalized and not by the constitution of investments, of risky Contracts which represent so many bills of exchange drawn on the future regarding which the slightest incident or any kind of invalidity can destroy everything.

Before 1972 a French footballer was bound to the club that signed him more securely than was ever the case in Britain. A player having signed a contract, was liable to find that he had by so doing bound himself to one club for a matter of twelve or thirteen years.

As the English Players' Union had done far back in time – in 1912 – in respect of L. J. Kingaby, the National Union chose one such case, that of Marius Tresor, of the Marseilles club A.C. Ajaccien, to contest in the courts. The aim was to nullify a contract that was counter to the law of the land in respect of industrial contractual obligations, and to enable Tresor 'to free himself' from being obliged to accept 'new ties of subordination of long duration which would deprive him for evermore of the fruit of his own work and of the freedom written into the constitution'.

Having succeeded in this instance (unlike the PU in 1912!) the National Union called for a show of solidarity and support from the other bodies – the PFA being one – belonging to the International Federation of Professional Footballers, FIFPRO. That this support was forthcoming from bodies in Britain, Italy, West Germany, Holland, Austria, and Portugal, shows a belief in international collaboration on one level that has not been treated with much interest by the ever avid media.

Contractual insecurity is one reason why players will not readily step out of line. But there are other ways of inducing a feeling of insecurity. When housing is difficult for so many young people, it is not surprising that the setting up of a footballer and his family in a 'club house' or 'club flat' arouses some envy. Yet, even though the accommodation provided may be excellent, it is still akin to the tied cottage.

*In the old days I was called a rebel. This more often than not was because I would insist that this or that was not right. I remember during the early part of my career what happened to players of my acquaintance whose careers with one club came to a sudden end. In the one case it was on account of injury. In the other it was because of the dislike of a manager. Both players were evicted from the club properties which they were occupying. This is the main reason for me always buying my own house. This gives some independence – a quality that I have always prized. I do not see why any player should be held over a barrel, which is liable to happen when he lives in a club property.*

In one sense every unmarried footballer has only himself to fend for. This is hardly ever realized by those who are the main critics of the profession. The 'loneliness of the long distance footballer' to which reference was made earlier has more than one meaning. Although he is taught to subordinate himself in many ways to the views and interests of others, when in action the player is quite isolated. So that one bad pass – one tiny error committed within the tenth part of a second – can prove disastrous. And there is only one person to blame! Of this the player is made well aware in every newspaper of the next few days.

Obviously because of the nature of the game each player has

his own individual problems to overcome as he has his own individual skills to give. All of this shows the difficulty in trying to assess the value of a player to the community, and how important it is to understand that no two players are alike.

The game, of course, is a team game, but as such it is the sum total of many highly personal contributions. Although some things change, some remain exactly the same. It was sickening inexplicably to lose one's form a hundred years ago. It still is. There is a permanent challenge to complacency in the fluctuations in one's popularity. Maybe this should not have any influence. But it does, for we are all human, while in any case popularity has to be paid for at a high price.

*Yesterday I met perhaps fifty children out in the country near Wolverhampton when I broke off, actually from working on this book, to draw raffle tickets for a charity. They all crowded round for an autograph. Next year I may not find so many autograph-hunters looking for me. The year after that there may be none at all. The career of a footballer is brutally short.*

*I always remember the wisdom of one old player. He was asked, 'Don't you get fed up signing autographs?' Then, after a pause, he said, 'When no one asks for your autograph that's the time to get fed up.'*

Since the abolition of the maximum wage the footballer has moved a little further up the social scale. Some have gone further up than others, and the attitudes of the public seem also to have changed. The average fan (if there is one) probably regards the top players with respect because of their evident material prosperity. He also mixes his respect with envy. The relationship between celebrity and public is an ambiguous one. The celebrity is allowed no privacy when he is up, and no mercy when he is down.

Footballers are sometimes easier to exploit than individualists in other professions because of their relative youthfulness. A youngster of twenty can be in the big money. There will be a lot of people only too anxious to help him get rid of it.

Where there is money there are parasites. Corruption in British football is infrequent – one might even say there is less of it than in most branches of life – and where it has been discovered it has been ruthlessly dealt with. Where it has occurred it has come not from within but from without as a general rule. That is, from people who thought that by exploiting footballers they could themselves benefit. In recent years some of these exploiters have done well in entertainment as agents. No sooner is a young star born than there is a galaxy of agents around him, all ready to help him – and themselves. There are, of course, good agents. But there are those who are less good, who look after other interests than those of their supposed clients.

The best bulwark we have against exploitation is the PFA and one cannot praise too highly the work of its present Secretary, Cliff Lloyd, and its small and dedicated staff as well as that of George Davies, the legal adviser, who is passionate about the fair treatment of the professional footballer. Between them they have solidified the structure of the PFA and helped us all to see that it has authority. It has above all been successful in helping all professional footballers to obtain better financial rewards.

The PFA is sometimes compared with the representative body of the actors – Equity. Three years ago Equity managed to negotiate a minimum weekly wage for an actor of £18. There are 21 000 members of Equity. The average number of weeks worked in a year is 14·5 for actors, 11·5 for actresses. There are stars who earn a lot, and the public makes its image of the actor out of the poster displays outside the theatres, the supposed glamour of the life, and the gossip columnists. For the rest they do not want to know. It was Sir Henry Irving who once said that 'the economics of the theatre are based on the fact that the average actor is unemployed'.

Football may not be as precarious as that, but falling attendances and the demise of less fashionable clubs may very easily increase the insecurity of players. The fact that there is security at all is due in large measure to the tenacity of the PFA.

*Now if footballers and actors are compared it will be pointed out that the latter often have strong views about the world's affairs, and that they are generally in the forefront of protest against unjust conditions wherever they may be found. Why is this not the case with professional footballers who, after all, mostly come out of backgrounds that can hardly be described as 'privileged'? One reason for the greater willingness of members of the theatrical profession to express their views is that they are much more masters of their own destiny. An actor does not have the FA, the Football League, a manager, a chairman, and a board of directors of a club breathing down his neck. An actor is less likely to be accused of lack of loyalty, or patriotism, or whatnot. We are back where we started – with 'loyalty' and 'honour' hung round our necks.*

There is an old cliché that sport and politics do not mix. Maybe they should not, and if it were left to the participants they would not. But alas, they do! There is no denying that the Olympic Games are almost entirely of political significance, nor that the World Cup is any different. In many countries there is a Ministry of Sport, which is naturally politically directed. In England we don't have quite that, but, headed by a second-rank Minister, a section of the Department of Education and Science. Outside of this there are many semi-voluntary and independent organizations linked with civic, regional and government departments in different ways.

*There is always the worry that sportsmen can be manipulated. There are plenty of people anxious to look after the consciences of others. But they do not always realize the pressures. An Irish player has many emotions within him and is more aware than most that for him the area of politics is just one huge minefield. Apart from the local matters about which one must think daily there are complications that arise in other spheres. I remember the time when Northern Ireland were in the World Cup Competition and playing in the same group as the Russians. In between matches with them the invasion of Czechoslovakia took place. Like many other people I objected to this. I thought about not taking part in the return match. I gave this a great deal of thought, and found myself in a cleft stick. If I didn't play I was weakening the Irish team and helping the Russians. Then I thought that the Russian players probably did not know what was going on anyway. In the end I played because I thought the best thing to happen was for the Russians to be beaten. That may be a very simple way of looking at the issue. But what does one do? The Press (with some exceptions) is generally advising sportsmen to keep their noses out of politics. But I don't have to say that*

*freedom of speech and opinion is what we are told to prize above every-
thing else. Why should footballers be denied this right?*

*Once again the bogey of insecurity comes up. The average life of a
footballer is eight years. One can find oneself an old man at twenty-eight.
(At my age I feel more like 100!) There is always the chance of
permanent injury. The manager can be sacked and his successor may
not like your face. One day you are in, the next you are out.*

*How aware is the public of the insecurity that haunts my colleagues?*

# 10. Thoughts on Rough Play

*'Who makes violence?'*

We may as well start with the first complaint of the ignorant. That is, that football is more violent than it ever was and that footballers are chiefly responsible. One might have said entirely responsible, except that referees come in for a share of blame. 'But what is needed', wrote a prominent journalist some time ago, 'is greater courage by referees to deal with the sinners.' Some unpleasant things do take place in football. But to be truthful the worst excesses are to be found outside the British Isles. And some players (they are well enough known) are inclined to throw their weight about without regard to the consequences either to themselves or their opponents. On the whole, and this could be argued from statistics, footballers do not condone violence any more than the next man, though from the way people talk it might seem that with the majority of them toughness is a way of life.

It is worth getting a few things straight right away. In one way or another we are all violent. The violence that is part of human nature has to be tamed. It can be tamed by consciously turning away from it. It can be got rid of. A footballer learns to turn away from violence simply because his livelihood depends on his being able to refrain from retaliating on someone who has either injured him or annoyed him. On the other hand he has the opportunity to get rid of some of his inborn tendencies to violence by the combat and physical conflict which is his profession. There is obviously a very thin borderline between what is fair and what is unfair. Thin, because defining what is in the one category and what is in the other is nearly impossible. You are sure you know a foul when you see one, but the person next to you at a game knows that what you consider a foul is certain not to be one. Of course, there is the referee's decision. But he is fallible, and must often try to discern the thought behind the deed.

On the whole professional footballers get on with each other pretty well, as well as members of any other professions from what we may notice, and with a good deal less backbiting and malicious gossip than goes on in some!

*Friendships that grow up within the game are different from most other kinds of friendship. Let me say at once, however, that there is a very strong bond between players because of the pressures of the game. The pressures are perhaps at their strongest when a player has left one club for another. He may have lost favour with the one crowd. He has to gain it all over again, with a new and usually very critical set of fans. This is where the sympathy of team-mates can be felt. Many of them have been through the same thing, and the way they show their sympathy is often one's only life-line. Bonds between players grow daily without anyone realizing that this is so.*

*After a bad game, missing an important goal or giving one away, being jeered by the home crowd – the most frightening and soul destroying experience; or after a confrontation with an aspiring new, keen manager; these are the times when one needs one's colleagues.*

*How much the pressure of the crowd makes for unity of sympathy I learned in my early days, when I was playing for Blackburn Rovers. I remember going over to Preston to see Blackpool v Preston. The legendary Stanley Matthews was in the Blackpool team, and from the time he entered the field until the final whistle the crowd never stopped hurling abuse.*

*When I think back on this I take the main reasons for their hurling abuse as (a) he did not play for Preston, (b) the media had the audacity to compare Stanley with Tom (Finney). But by the way he played it seemed that the old master had ear-plugs! From that night onwards playing in front of hostile crowds ceased to be an ordeal for me. Now I would say that the more they banter the better! All of this reminds me of an old Greek saying: 'A man who does not suffer does not learn.'*

*In any amateur game the social side should be, and is, important. It should not be neglected in the professional game.*

*In the normal League club – the real fraternizing is done in the directors' lounge and in the board-room. I have always had the impression*

H

*that the last people to be thought of in a personal capacity at the head-quarters of a football club are the players.*

*It is not surprising that players rarely see the inside of a board-room as guests of their employers. Here, however, I must be fair to Wolves. I have been in the board-room at Molineux more than I have been anywhere else. The chairman, John Ireland, has worked hard to make the playing staff feel a sense of belonging, so we have not had the same kind of alienation that can unfortunately be found elsewhere. I must say that when players are invited into the board-room for a drink – after some important match say, against a foreign team – they do appreciate the pleasure of mixing with friends of the club and civic notabilities.*

*One understandably makes friends in the profession because one plays alongside people in club or international football. But it is not easy to make friends with people in other teams. If one plays for a club in a large city, however, there is usually at least one other club whose players one can meet socially. So far as I am concerned, whenever I have played at Hampden Park in an international match it has always been a pleasure to mix with the Scots after the game. But this is most unusual; indeed, in my experience of internationals, it is unique.*

*A normal fixture does not provide opportunity to meet one's friends and colleagues in the opposing side as one would very much like to do. There is a chance of passing one or two words before the start of a match. There may be half an hour afterwards. It is, it should be remembered, only in the last few years that a players' tea-room has become part of the amenities of the average club, where after the game players on both sides can wet their whistles. To class some of these tea-rooms among the amenities sometimes calls for some exercise of the imagination! In my early days someone used to bring a dozen bottles of beer and a bottle of sherry into the dressing-room after the match.*

*It really is unfortunate that as things are there is not much opportunity to mix after a game. Within three-quarters of an hour after an away game has finished the team is usually on its way home.*

*A lot of players, then, only get to know each other through the media, and very often they get entirely the wrong impression. This always reminds me of the old saying: reputation is what people think you are, while not knowing you for what you are.*

*The PFA now has its own 'Player of the Year' award, to be conferred on one of their number by the players themselves. This serves a number of purposes. It draws attention to the qualities which players regard most highly in their colleagues. It provides opportunity for players to mix socially. We have on this occasion three or four hundred players, representatives of all the League clubs, and they can find out what they have in common. The only other time we can meet all together is for the Annual General Meeting of the PFA. These meetings, as well as courses that are developing under the direction of Bob Kerry, the Education Officer of the PFA, all have their place in encouraging the sense of responsibility that alone is the guarantee of true discipline.*

*The 'violent players' you may read about in the Sunday papers you would not be able to recognize as such if you came across them unawares in the street, or in a hotel. Of course, players do have a go at one another from time to time on the field and the crowd howls for the blood or the head of the one they don't like. But when the final whistle goes and the confrontation of the game stops any idea of malice that may have been there during the ninety minutes ceases – except for some echoes in the bathroom! One forgets everything except, perhaps, the knocks that one has taken. Spectators find it hard to understand this. It is well known that crowd confrontation lasts a lot longer than that between players.*

Quite a deal of the violence that is talked about is within the mind of the observer. It is a hard thought, but what does the average man or woman do towards reducing or even condemning the violence that is in the world – to children, to underprivileged people, to animals, to nature – except talk – and not always that. There are those who not only do not condemn violence, they actively look for it – and this fact has brought a lot of money to a lot of people.

Violence on the football field is only deplorable, and every responsible player would say so. But the attitude of the well-heeled spectators or even non-spectators (not the pathetic, usually undernourished, casualties of society who are invariably called hooligans, who do come to football matches) who secretly enjoy a punch-up, yet who are the first to demand that players should be sent off, are more deplorable. Among these good people are a fair number who are quick to subscribe to the opinion that bad behaviour on the terraces is sparked off by what happens on the field. However, it seems that for the time being at least the soccer hooligan phase is over and that scapegoats for hooliganism must be found somewhere else than among professional footballers. But while it was at its height the campaign of innuendo against a whole profession was very unpleasant. It was, indeed, a smear campaign of the worst sort.

It may be said that footballers should learn to take the rough with the smooth, and not be sensitive to criticism. It is by no means certain that they are over sensitive in this respect, but there are some things that one should not be asked to take.

It was an article by a lady journalist, Anne Edwards, of the *Sunday Express*, that rubbed us up the wrong way. This no doubt admirable woman began a piece in this way: 'Strewth, how can I face the months ahead, the hours and hours of highly paid publicized thuggery called football? Do you realize that we are in for nine whole months of brawling, kicking, cheating, shamming from the players?' All right. This is only hysteria. But if a footballer showed that degree of hysteria he would be got rid of as a liability. If Miss (or Mrs) Edwards were to substantiate her views (which can hardly be described as an argument) she would have to name names. And then there would be trouble. It is safe to shoot untruths at abstracts. It is also cowardly. A good case can be made out for stating that quite contrary to popular journalistic opinion football is much less violent than it used to be. And it is played a lot more.

It is the professional teams which get all the publicity. But even when one adds in all the minor professional leagues these teams numerically are not very significant. There are 33 000 amateur clubs which are affiliated to the FA and taking part in organized competitions. There are 14 000 schools in the Schools' Football Associations. Before anyone says again that football is more violent than it was it must be looked at in whole and not just in part.

History has some horrifying episodes placed within the game. At the very beginning of the thirteenth century a young Englishman was set on and killed during a football game in Oxford by some Irish students. There is no doubt that this was part of the eternal Anglo-Irish argument which plagues us to this day and not really of the game itself. But the death of this student is put down to the violence of the game rather than of the conditions and prejudices of the time. Almost exactly five hundred years ago football was written of as 'more common, undignified, and worthless than any other kind of game'. In 1540 Sir Thomas Elyot, in a notorious passage, wrote that there was 'nothing but beastly fury, and extreme violence' in the game. A certain amount of 'fury and violence' lies at the roots of football, if only because it is a game of physical contact played at speed. Where it is played before a crowd of spectators it is seen as a symbol of the contrasting loyalties of the home and away elements among the spectators. But ever since football became organized the trend has been to increase the precautions against it becoming rough.

The great age of football legislation was the nineteenth century, and the first attempts to codify rules were made in the schools that belonged to the well-to-do. Compulsory education did not come in until 1870 so the kind of people who considered leisure pursuits like football were very restricted in experience and outlook. This is what the 'best people' thought of as refinement in football in 1845 in certain of the rules drawn up at Rugby School:

XIV.  No hacking with the heel, or unless below the knee is fair.
XV.  No one wearing projecting nails or iron plates on the soles or heels of his shoes or boots shall be allowed to play . . .
XXII.  A player standing up to another may hold one arm only, but may hack him or knock the ball out of his hand if he attempts to kick it, or go beyond the line of touch.

Periodically the game that supposedly had been started at Rugby School, some twenty years before this attempt at rule making, draws devotees to Rugby to pay tribute to the founders of their game.

But not everyone, even in those days, was prepared to go along with such licensed excess of vigour. In 1863 the new Football Association took the historic decision to do away with 'hacking and kicking', as a result of which football split into two parts. On the one side there was football, a 'dribbling game', approved by the Association – hence 'soccer'. On the other side, after the kind of game approved at Rugby School, there was the 'handling code'. That division was caused by differing views as to what was and what was not violent, and as to what was manly and what was not. There was, of course, a lot of humbug. This was created by the English tendency to turn everything into a moral issue. Everything, no doubt, can be seen as a moral issue, but there is nothing but trouble when there are varying standards of moral judgment.

Our kind of football suffers in public because a different set of values is consulted from those which operate in some other spheres. The really ideal game, it was once suggested, was cricket. A very good game it is, but in ideas neither better nor worse than most others. However, it has always had the quality Press, and more than its fair share of famous writers, behind it. And yet there is a nasty record of brutality in it. The term 'brutal' is usually avoided, but 'bodyline', as applied to bowling, is not. In one form or another this kind of attack on the person now belongs to the pattern of the game. And the decorous crowds (let alone the less decorous ones) that used to watch the first class game liked nothing better than a fast bowler sending down, and then up, bouncers. Some fast bowlers got into trouble with the Press, but they were usually from overseas. That is, since the time of Larwood and Voce, and their uncompromising captain, Jardine.

Soccer is played in a large number of schools. In some schools, however, rugby football is preferred. That is fair enough – if it is genuinely felt that this type of game is a better exercise and enjoyment for boys. It is disturbing though to find out that there is sometimes more to it than this. The negative reason for encouraging rugby football is that a particular class of people is supposed both to play and to patronize soccer. Although this is far from the truth it is still maintained by those who dislike the look of facts. So the myth gets around that rugby football is a better game because (to be blunt) better people superintend it, play it, and support it. This *is* myth because in Ireland, Wales and Scotland especially many people do play the game simply because they prefer it.

One myth breeds another. An amateur game is supposed to be better than a professional game because it is amateur. As it stands that is nonsense. Its implications are more disturbing, for we are brought back to the essence of amateurism.

Sometimes one wonders whether the amateur game has

advanced very far beyond 1845. In 1972 the New Zealanders sent over a good-will mission in the form of the All Blacks. At the end of October 1972 the All Blacks played against Llanelli. In the record book Llanelli won. In the history of sport rugby football lost:

It would be idle to suggest that the play that followed was beautiful. Often it was ugly. Tempers were lost, fists were flung, and the boot was used for kicking men and for trampling.

*( The Guardian)*

A few days later the same All Blacks played against Cardiff:

Hard play is acceptable, but when players refuse to take hard knocks and retaliate with fist and boot, they must be sent off . . .

The game reached its unpleasant climax when Matheson, the All Black prop, was laid out cold with a terrific uppercut five minutes after half-time . . .

*( The Observer)*

On a foggy day at Cardiff Arms Park the All Blacks played against East Glamorgan:

. . . the All Blacks scrum-half and vice-captain let go with a couple of flaming punches . . . Evans had to leave the field with a badly split lip and was later taken to hospital for stitches.

*( The Sunday Times)*

All of this may have been condoned on the grounds that this is the way the New Zealanders like it at home. ('And let's not be proud, Mr Kirkpatrick,' wrote Hunn in *The Observer*, 'that it's even rougher in New Zealand.') But when, at an earlier stage of the same season Pontypool played Cardiff:

. . . there was a flurry of punches . . . during which the Pontypool prop forward . . . was laid out. He was carried off on a stretcher and taken to the Royal Gwent Hospital, Newport, with suspected rib injuries.

*( The Guardian)*

Very well, this is Wales. But it was the game in general that came in for this criticism in *The Observer* (11 November, 1972):

Far more people watched the leading rugby match of the day than the leading soccer match, and what a charmer it was. It's three weeks since we asked why rugby referees were not doing the job properly and sending off offensive brawlers.

Two got the boot at Blackheath [a top London club], but why none at Cardiff? Why none at Old Deer Park [where Richmond, another top London club, play], where the *Guardian* man commented firmly that the time was not far off when, if violence were not curbed, somebody was going to get killed?

Most of us who love rugby have the scars to prove it. But let's not excuse vicious ill-tempered hooliganism with this manly phrase, 'It's a contact sport'.

The psychological implications of all this must be left to others to analyse. All that is of concern here is that in the true blue amateur branch of football, rugby football that is, violence is by no means uncommon. And yet, apart from a few affronted critics in the quality papers, nobody denounces the players or the game, nobody gives this form of violence as a cause of contemporary moral decline, while some armchair critics, at least implicitly, praise it.

In soccer there has been a progressive tightening of control on rough behaviour. From 1871 jostling was only permitted when a player to be jostled was facing his own goal. Eight years later, jumping into a tackle was disallowed. In 1907 a further attempt to reduce tension on the field came in the form of a ban on 'violent or dangerous' jostling. In 1950 it was required that in a sliding tackle the ball must be seen to have been the object of the tackle. When in 1971 further tightening of the rules was enjoined there were quite a number of people who still protested that the game was getting too soft.

*I certainly would not say that, but to get things in perspective, it should be understood that when people talk about a hard player or a player who is 'afraid to get stuck in' they are talking about other people, not mere objects. When writers go on about roughness and violence they do not speak with the authority of having done a statistical count of their own injuries to prove whatever they want to prove. So far as I am concerned, after seventeen years at the top I really believe that rough play has decreased rather than increased. This may seem a startling* thing to say. I have had a lot of kicks, but not severe enough to miss many matches. Most of my injuries I have suffered by myself. I broke an ankle at Portsmouth in August 1957. That was no one's fault. But since it was not discovered for nearly three months I had more cause to complain of negligence than the cause of the injury. In 1970 there was an accidental clash of heads at Everton with Keith Newton which made me miss four months. Apart from those there have been pulled muscles and occasional bruises.

It would be interesting to take a count of the number of players injured any week in the forty-six League matches played. One should then compare this number with that of players injured in other ways. For instance, quite a number of injuries are sustained in training and in practice matches. Others occur at home or when players get out of their cars. What is alarming, of course, is the number of ordinary people who are injured in unnecessary ways – but that is another matter.

I used to say that a good groundsman was as useful to a club as a star player. The same goes for a physiotherapist, and in this respect there has been a tremendous advance in knowledge and skill. This is another aspect of the game in which Leeds United have played a leading role.

As a matter of fact evidence of the Leeds search for perfection is shown by the insistance of the club's medical officer, Dr Ian Adams, that standards in the treatment of sporting injuries should be raised all over Britain. Treatment methods applied to professionals, from which much has been learned, could certainly be applied to amateur sport with the most beneficial results. In August 1973 an injury clinic was opened in Leeds, where 540 cases were treated in one year. About 50 per cent were soccer players, 30 per cent rugby players, and 15 per cent athletes.

In England I think I can say that today's footballers are more thoughtful for players in an opposing team than at previous times in the game's history. The media may suggest otherwise, but I judge from the field and not from the commentator's box.

With the game abroad it is sometimes different. I have never experienced anything like a game against Lazio in the Anglo-Italian tournament – a tournament I would never take part in again. I also remember a World Cup qualifying match against Turkey. Here there really was brutality and violence: kicking, deliberate provocation, spitting – which to me is the lowest form of misdemeanour, quite intentional punching while corners were being taken. All this was in front of a referee who *did nothing. In England there are people who say that our game is violent, dirty, and so on. Honestly I don't think it has ever been cleaner. I am not trying to say that our national game is full of saints. We do have offenders and black sheep, but which industry doesn't? And there are a whole lot of players who are among the most courageous playing anywhere.*

*Since I came over from Ireland soccer has become less physical; some people are hell bent on taking all of the bodily contact out of the game. This leads us to the subject of discipline, which will be dealt with in some detail.*

*Before considering the subject of discipline, however, the reader should first of all think how much discipline **he** needs, and who it is that keeps on shouting the word at footballers. So far as rough play in the sense of violent play is concerned he should rely on the evidence of his own eyes.*

*Some of the media experts we have around today would find violence at a vicarage tea-party. It makes news.*

# 11. Discipline

*'Why is it that we professional footballers
are told to have more control over **our**
emotions?'*

*When I was a teenager I went to Wembley, to see Bolton play Man-
chester United in the emotion-charged Cup Final of 1958. I remember
how Harry Gregg seemed to have the ball and suddenly Nat Lofthouse
came charging in. Gregg lost the ball, which was bunged over the line,
and the referee gave a goal. Since 1971 no referee would have allowed
this goal.*

The official account of this incident (Bolton were one goal
up at the time) is sufficiently vivid to quote. The words capture
the skill of the movement leading to this climax as well as the
vigour of the climax. But the vigour goes by as unremarkable;
no question here of unfairness:

. . . Holden, on the Bolton left wing, swung a low ball across the
edge of the Manchester penalty-area, Stevens jumped over it as it
came and let it run on to Hennin. He immediately reversed the
direction of the move by stabbing the ball back to Stevens who had
run into the unmarked inside-left position. Stevens crashed in a
terrific shot from barely twelve yards range, but somehow Gregg
got his hands there and pushed it over his head high into the air.
He turned to catch it as it fell, but Lofthouse, quick to follow up as
ever, was on hand to charge both goalkeeper and ball into the net
to put Bolton two up.

*In contrast to this we may consider what happened at St Andrew's,
Birmingham, on 29 December 1973, when Birmingham City played
Leeds. The score was one – nil in favour of the home team. A high cross
was fired in from the left, and David Harvey, the Leeds goalkeeper,
came to catch it, when a local hero – Bob Latchford, a bearded and
burly striker – barged into him. The goalie fumbled and the ball just
rolled into the net. Utter confusion broke out. The referee gave a goal*

*amid the disbelief of an aggrieved Leeds team and Harvey lay prostrate. To add to the confusion the linesman had his flag up. In the end the decision was reversed and the goal disallowed. It should be added that the unfortunate referee that day was not one with vast experience.*

*I have seen old film clips where goalkeepers would go down at the feet of oncoming forwards. This required a lot of guts. Particularly as the forwards would often kick through and usually trample all over the goalkeeper. You don't see this today, nor do you see the good old-fashioned shoulder charge. This is something about which I would probably like to challenge referees and football authorities. I am all for taking unfair physical contact out of the game, but there is a place for fair physical contact. I really can't see the objection to charging a goalkeeper shoulder to shoulder when he has both his feet on the ground.*

*I was playing against Liverpool a year ago, and I challenged Ray Clemence in the first few minutes of the game. It was a fair charge, shoulder to shoulder, but the referee came running over to me. 'Derek, cut it out,' he said, 'you know I won't stand for that – one more time and I will have to book you!' I agree with Bill McGarry that if the people who make the rules succeed in taking physical contact out of the game they will remove a great deal of the game itself.*

*It is sometimes said, and I am sometimes asked, if managers are the cause of dirty play. The answer to this is that there is a problem of understanding (in vogue language, a problem of communication). Once a player becomes a full time player he receives instructions every day of his life. Under these conditions one can become brain-washed and indoctrinated, so that in the end a player can take what a manager says in a quite literal sense. I am sure that no director would put any kind of pressure on managements to resort to rough tactics. In many cases one finds that a director has put his foot down, that a board has given proof of its wish to eliminate any rough behaviour on the field by clear instructions, if there is feeling that the name of the club is being tarnished. To their credit the boards and managements of our clubs do still value their standing in football circles. There are, as we all know and as I have already indicated, some players who have a mean streak, some who have a stronger will to win than others, and some who do not dare to think of defeat. In saying this we are only saying that footballers are human.*

*In a recent issue of a magazine for football coaches, the referee Gordon Hill did suggest that managers and coaches had something to answer for. What he wrote is, of course, his own personal opinion, but because of his experience both within the game and outside (he is a high school headmaster) it deserves to have due attention paid to it. 'Managers and coaches,' he said, 'are making the most extraordinary physical and mental demands on players. Intense coaching produces an emotional response, often violent and unscrupulous. Put one man against another, constantly drive both towards ever-increasing limits of performance and it is inevitable that violence and cheating will occur.'*

*The note of warning here sounded applies to those outside the game who are ultimately responsible, even though indirectly, for what goes on within it. And in these days what applies to one game applies to all.*

*When I was a lad we never bothered with rules and regulations. We knew what was fair and what was unfair. I played many games without referees or linesmen and we managed to discipline ourselves quite tolerably.*

*The pity is, I suppose, that the word discipline has taken on such a repressive meaning in football. Footballers who agree among themselves about what is permissible and what is not, now find that they are hedged in with restrictions that are often meaningless. They also feel at times that they are being regarded as delinquents.*

In an extreme form this attitude was written into the March issue of the *FA News*, 1970, by A. H. Fabian – an amateur member of the Derby County side of forty years ago: 'As a result of watching a considerable amount of League football it is becoming increasingly apparent to me that "crime" in football is paying.' That, it may be thought, was pitching it a good deal too high. In any case to introduce the word 'crime' was distinctly emotive. That is part of the problem – the language used against footballers.

*One instance of the power of the word is the increasing use of the term 'professional foul'. There is truly no such thing. A foul is a foul. Or rather, a foul is a foul when the referee says it is – not when another player says it is, and not when the crowd swears it is. A 'professional foul', as the media call it, I have known ever since I started to kick a ball. It is, in short, a deliberate foul, and to call it 'professional' is merely another subtle way to write down the status of the professional.*

*One might be inclined to shout back 'amateur foul' sometimes. If anyone wants to know what that is, it is the kind of foul common in an amateur game presumably. For further information on that head turn back to pages 117–120!*

*The wide meaning given to 'professional foul' brings in obstruction, tripping, pulling, holding, handling. At its most professional the 'professional foul' stops one from scoring a goal. A recent example was Roy McFarland's celebrated foul during the 1973 game between England and Poland at Wembley. I once had just such a foul against me when Larry Lloyd of Liverpool brought me down with a similar kind of rugby tackle. This kind of foul is spectacular and brings a great weight of accusation from commentators. One may wonder from all the publicity given to particular incidents how much of this sort of thing goes on. Well, this depends on the kind of match it is, but taking the whole range of matches played during a season not all that much. What happens is that the tension-filled European or World competition match, backed by hidden nationalistic feelings, gets out of hand and players who are pretty nervous to start with behave in an abnormal manner. Crowds do not always help.*

*But at the centre of the disciplinary matter is always the referee. In international competitions it is my experience that the referee is in most cases in favour of the home side. The simplest way of gauging this tendency is to examine where the balance lies in respect of penalties. An away side that gets a penalty awarded against the home side is double blessed – to get a penalty and (hopefully) a bonus away goal. There are certain grounds where one feels that discrimination takes place in favour of the home team. In the old days this was true of Old Trafford. Today it is felt about Anfield. Or there may seem to be extra consideration for a team during a record breaking run. There is nothing deliberate. It is simply that subconscious forces take control.*

*At home we have good referees and some less good referees, but it is always the referee who determines at any time what the law actually is. In the present situation a front man may not challenge a goalkeeper. If he does, nine times out of ten he will be penalized. More than that, the referee will probably have some harsh words to say to the player. That is my experience.*

*There is no doubt that after the tightening up that was decreed in August 1971 the rules were interpreted in a different light from previously. It was obvious that referees had become more strict, and that they were now observing the letter of the law – the law in fact being everything that the Football League laid down.*

There are complaints sometimes that players appeal too often. In this matter, at any rate, players have tradition on their side. In looking more closely at this we find ourselves meeting the referee's function within its historical context.

The first official (or semi-official) suggestion that a referee was needed in football came four hundred years ago! The schoolmaster Richard Mulcaster, writing in the time of Queen Elizabeth I, observed that at any game there should be standing by one person 'which can judge of the play, and is judge over the parties, and hath authority to command in the place . . .' Schoolmasters have played an important part in refereeing ever since. Sir Stanley Rous, for example, was a schoolmaster and a referee once upon a time. Two other schoolmasters to gain prominence in modern football as referees are Ken Aston and Gordon Hill.

When football became more or less institutionalized a hundred years ago the rules were interpreted by two umpires (as in cricket), each responsible for one half of the field. In cases of doubt the umpires deferred to the judgment of a third official – the referee. In the beginning football was expected to go on more or less of its own accord. The umpires did nothing until they were asked to intervene. Players, therefore, were both entitled and expected to appeal. The parallel with cricket is clear. The only remaining matter to arouse interest is the manner in which an appeal is made. There is nothing contrary to the spirit of the game (to which people always refer when they can't think of any other source of authority) in the appeal itself.

History helps to get many things into perspective. In 1931 and 1932 Stanley Rous was asked to take charge of the Oxford–Cambridge matches. This was because play in these fixtures had deteriorated to a point that gave grave concern to all those who had the interests of the amateur game at heart at that time. The game had developed into a rough-and-tumble, because players and spectators (when there were any) objected to it being held up by the referee's whistle. It was suggested that this was what was wrong with the professional game at that time. However – and there is a nice irony in this in view of what he wrote 39 years later (see p. 125) – the Cambridge captain, A. H. Fabian 'with the hearty concurrence of W. H. Bradshaw, his opposite number, wrote to the Football Association and asked them especially to provide a referee who would control the game with strict regard for the rules, and would penalize sternly any unnecessary rough play'.

*The unfortunate referee seems always to have been a focal figure for argument. I have sometimes wondered that would happen if there were no officials. It is a nice thought and even though it is impracticable one wonders whether the game would be reduced to a shambles, or whether it could run under a communal consent to observe the agreed principles. After all, as a boy in Belfast I played often enough in games that had no referee, that were hard and vigorous, yet were still not undisciplined. As a footnote to this it is worth remarking that we often play five- or six-a-side games in training. For these games we have neither referee nor trouble!*

In the earlier part of the century the referee's position was more or less secure. Unless he was quite hopeless he was protected to a large extent by his office. As with players the old masters tend to loom over us much larger than life, partly because there is a frequent tendency to romanticize over the past, but more especially because they actually did have more power on account of the way in which society was organized. It was a hierarchic system for the most part, and the referee was well up in the hierarchy.

J. T. Howcroft, of Bolton, refereed his first league match at the age of twenty in 1894. He took charge of his last match after he was fifty and he had been on the active list of referees for twenty-eight full seasons. (Nowadays a referee – however good – is compulsorily retired at forty-seven.)

A story told of 'J.T.' in a Crewe Alexandra programme of fifty years ago gives some idea of his prestige:

Imagine Season 1922–3. Two First League contestants, one side the Spurs, [J.] Banks, the old outside right careering along with the ball. Full back of the opposing side fouls Banks rather badly.

He comes to earth rather heavily, up he jumps, arm raised to strike the delinquent. Just at that moment a whistle blows, and Master Banks, very much like a school-boy before the master, remembers that football's the game, not fisticuffs.

When Howcroft went to referee at Crewe for the first (and probably the last) time, the directors of what was then the bottom club in the league hoped that they had not forgotten the elements of true sportsmanship and that the supporters would not fail in their duty: 'Usually the crowd [on any ground] pay their token respect to this "great official" by giving him a heartier cheer than they usually extend to their team!'

Within the game the referee is absolutely supreme. He alone knows at any moment what the laws are, for he determines what they are according to the words in which they are embedded and according to the significance of those words within a particular context. The referee is the timekeeper. Whatever anything else may record it is the referee's watch that brings a match to an end. In a paper prepared for the Birmingham University Centre for Contemporary Cultural Studies in 1971 Mr C. R. Critcher wrote:

The recognition is . . . that some form of arbitrary authority is necessary; the game could not go on without a referee and may be reduced to a shambles if one side consistently and completely defies his authority. The similarities between the role of the referee and those of the policeman and schoolteacher, are obvious. Just as they are derided and evaded, so is the referee often interpreted by both sides and their supporters as the legitimate butt for all their frustrations. There is never any suggestion that any better form of authority might be designed, only that existing authority is to be undermined as far as possible without destroying its base.

*A major problem we face today is the inability of referees and players to communicate with each other properly. In the days of Howcroft, although players were more accustomed to obey hard and fast rules and disciplines, this problem was not so acute. This was because the pressures on both parties were less.*

*A main reason for our problem today is that players and referees are forbidden to mix before games. Over the years I have made numerous*

I

*attempts to be more than polite before the start of a game. Unfortunately for both parties there has not been much of a response from the man in charge. After all these years I can quite clearly see that this has been a real stumbling-block. I am sorry to say that the gap between player and referee has widened considerably. Should you greet any of the officials he always gives the impression that he is looking over his shoulder to see if anyone is watching. This, of course, is not the case with every referee. I have got to know some of them quite well, and these are the ones who give a more positive response.*

*As soon as the final whistle has been blown it gives these referees, it seems, a sense of relief. It's not uncommon for them then to come into the dressing-room. Many a time I have been accosted by one of them with, 'If I go home to my twelve-year-old lad without your autograph I'll get shot!' One can hardly refuse the request!*

*The average referee tends, I think, to feel he is the victim of the show. He is never asked for his autograph! Or if he is I have never witnessed it. He has a certain kind of complex to start with, wondering maybe whether he is human or not. By most supporters he is seen as a necessary evil. Mr Critcher describes him as something between a policeman and a schoolteacher. To me it seems he is for the average supporter nearer to being a kind of traffic warden. Now players do not get to know referees as people, and referees do not get to know players. Their only contact is on the pitch iself. So the player (and a good many supporters) sees the referee as a shit who has never made a right decision in his life, and the referee sees most players as contrary buggers who won't accept his decision. Altogether referees see us, the players, as overgrown schoolboys, argumentative and behaving like prima donnas.*

*In August 1971, as we have stated, there was what has been called a purge. Here, again, we find a very strong word applied to a certain situation, and because the strong word was used everyone assumed it was the right word. This is another example of media influence. And describing what happened in 1971 as a purge slanted sympathy away from players and towards the strict disciplinarians who run around seeing what there is to crack down on! The avowed aim of the 1971 operation was to eliminate violence from football.*

This should be seen in context. In 1968 there was an article on 'International Football Law and Lawlessness' in the *FA Year Book*. Beginning with a dispute at the International Court at

The Hague that had nothing to do with football and referring to referee Rudolph Kreitlein's dismissal of the Argentinian Rattin from the 1966 England–Argentine World Cup match at Wembley, the article came to the conclusion that 'violence on the field is related to terrorism off it, and vice versa'. In fact there is no hard evidence to support this conclusion at all. But, nonetheless, the supposition that there was was good enough to continue the argument to this point: 'the increase of crime throughout the land in no way diminishes the disrepute into which football in England is dragged by the acts of its criminals on and off the field of play.'

Having thus established that there are 'criminals' on the field and by not naming them (for obvious reasons) the writer of this article made it certain that *all* players would come in for harsh comment. The odds now being against the players we have this pious injunction: 'What is now required at all levels of the game is an awareness that those who break the laws of football on the field and the laws of society off it should be branded equally as criminals and wrong-doers.' The call was a clear one: law and order. And football players stood there as potential, or indeed in some eyes actual, law breakers. It has already been noted on p. 116 that the calumny was catching.

*During 1971 secret meetings were held up and down the country amongst Football League administrators and referees. The outcome was confusion and chaos, which could have been avoided if all the club managers could have been consulted beforehand. There were bookings galore (1000 in the first few weeks of the 1971–2 season), very many for trivial misdemeanours. None of this did the image of the referee any good. The unfairness of it all was that the referees had no idea what they were letting themselves in for.*

*In my view they were being used to clean up all of society. The football legislators wanted to give a lead, to react to adverse publicity on the 'permissive society' and on the supposed decline in the standards of the youth of the country. Somewhere at this time I felt that if some of our administrators and legislators could have had football played without players they would do so.*

One first class referee, Danny Lyden, left the game because

of what happened at the time of the purge. He gave his reasons in the *Sports Argus*, of 29 January 1972. According to Lyden, referees had no choice during the great clean-up. The referee was watched from the stand at every match by an assessor. The first idea of having assessors was to form a panel of experienced men who would be able to help younger and less experienced referees. Within a couple of years, however, the number of assessors had outgrown the supply of competent men and some two-thirds were ex-linesmen. 'Armed with a list of 30 points to look for, they control the destiny of today's top-line referees. If it wasn't so tragic it would be laughable!'

Lyden made one other point of great importance, that it is out of place for a top administrator to make a hostile comment concerning a particular performance by a particular referee to the Press. Commonsense demands that dirty play shall be dealt with, but with justice. 'As far as I am concerned,' wrote Lyden, 'the main function of the referee is to control the game and the player with the minimum of intrusion. If he does this, most other comment is superfluous.'

Both players and referees recognize that both must co-exist. The best way of ensuring that this is a profitable and even harmonious state is for some sort of dialogue to be initiated. One of the advantages of having vocational or professional organizations is that dialogue can be conducted in a business-like manner. It is, therefore, to be hoped that the mooted exchange of views between the Association of Football League Referees and Linesmen, and the PFA, can lead to a fuller understanding of the problems faced by members of both bodies.

Football is a much more complex organization than appears on the surface. This is not least obvious in respect of the maintenance of discipline on the official level. This covers the widest possible range for, not only players, officials, and directors of clubs are under official jurisdiction, but also spectators. For instance a club is obliged by the rules of the FA to 'prevent betting and the use of objectionable language'. But it is clearly open to different tribunals to give differing interpretations of what is, and what is not 'objectionable language'. Once again we find ourselves up against the fact that while rules exist they may be variously applied. When rules are laid down it is im-

plicit that breaking them brings in certain sanctions. Sanctions
are punitive, and here again the matter of degree of severity is
a matter of interpretation.

A player is subject to club discipline in that a manager may
suspend him, or fine him, more or less arbitrarily. A player may
be thus disciplined either 'in his own interest' or in the interest
of the club. The more notable causes of managerial discipline
are speedily headlined. Whether it is fair to pillory a player in
this manner is a matter of opinion.

*In the event of a player being required to appear before a disciplinary
committee, however, his manager becomes his friend. This is a point at
which the player needs his friends. From the moment at which a booking
for a serious misdemeanour (in the referee's eyes) takes place the process
develops remorselessly. After a booking the player and the manager
discuss the situation, and await the referee's report which goes both to
club and player. There is a further conference and it is decided whether
to ask for a personal hearing or – presuming nothing can be achieved
by this means – to let the matter go to the disciplinary committee as it
stands.*

*A player who is called before a disciplinary committee finds himself
overwhelmed by unfamiliar and forbidding conditions. The members of
the committee are elderly – sometimes very elderly – and awe-inspiring.
They represent the FA and the League and are invested with considerable
authority. Essentially this is a private court rather like the Church
Courts that maintained their own ideas and standards of justice centuries ago. There is no doubt that the disciplinary committee members are
dedicated to the game. But – even though there may be a lawyer among
them – they are not legally trained. More importantly they have re-
straints on their impartiality. A committee member belongs to a club and
in this capacity he has prejudices against other clubs. He may dislike a
chairman or a manager of another club and when faced with a player
from that club at a hearing experience some difficulty in suppressing his
private feelings. It is small wonder that when sentences for the same
offence vary in the magistrates' courts the same thing takes place in the
restricted area of football offences. But it is not justice that discrepancies
should occur.*

*After the trauma of 1971 some reforms did take place. Principal
among these was the setting up of an Appeals Tribunal, the result of an*

*approach made by the management committee of the PFA to the Minister of State, Paul Bryan, and the Minister of Sport, Eldon Griffiths. The first important reform was the establishment of an Appeals Tribunal – to which players might refer their cases – consisting of nominees of the FA and the PFA with an independent chairman. In the first place the Chairman was Sir John Lang, the Government's Adviser on Sport.*

*Already this tribunal, on which representatives of the PFA have been Stanley Cullis, Bill Slater, and Tom Finney, has done good work in reviewing cases. One wonders whether it would not be better to have such a body acting in the first instance – as a disciplinary committee. The fact that there should be some sort of body is not disputed, for football is in the final issue too involved to have such matters left entirely to self-discipline and chance. Self-discipline is, of course, the foundation of good order, and so far as players are concerned any disciplinary authority should make the inculcation of self-control its first aim. This brings up the question as to what sort of body can best do this. The answer is, one that inspires confidence and commands cooperation as well as respect. A disciplinary committee could well consist of a representative of the PFA – an ex-player or an ex-manager, for instance – and a representative of the referees, with an independent chairman. This would be very much like the Appeals Tribunal which deals with the contracts of players who are in dispute with their clubs. Ideally there should be one body of this kind which would hold hearings in different centres and would be in a much better position to rationalize procedures and penalties.*

*The second significant innovation has been the introduction of the points system. This was brought into being at the same meeting on 19 May 1972, which gave us the Appeals Tribunal, and like it was provisional and subject to annual review – at least for the time being. The points system which evaluates offences on a 1–4 scale with automatic suspension for an aggregate of 12 points (subject to appeal), has the great merit that it leaves a player knowing where he stands. This certainly now makes for the feeling that fair play is a principle to be respected off the field as well as on it.*

*After playing through a season consisting of more than sixty matches, those who go right through without incurring any sort of reprimand are to be admired for self-control.*

# 12. Sponsorship, Public Relations, and Community Values

*'Going, going, gone?'*

In a famous article written in 1967 after the famous game (though that is the last word to apply) between Glasgow Celtic and the Racing Club of Argentine, Geoffrey Green summarized the situation in these words: 'At the root of all the evil is money, greed for power, the size of the rewards and the penalty for failure. No one can afford to lose any more.' All of this may be agreed to. But out of it come other questions. Whose money? Whose power? What rewards? And who pays the penalty for failure at the end of the affair?

The last question is the easiest to answer, for in the end it is the player who has to take the rap. It is true that managers and directors are not immune from criticism when things go wrong, and occasionally they may even find themselves in confrontation with angry supporters. But a manager who is fired is generally able to laugh all the way to his next assignment, for the kind of golden handshake allowed to one of management's failures seems sometimes to make failure even more worthwhile than success. This is not to say that managers do not deserve a great deal more support than they often receive, nor that they are frequently the victims of injustice.

The amateur director of a club normally only has some of his pocket money at stake – sometimes not even this. There are board-room problems from time to time and sometimes powerful shareholders, or groups of shareholders, stage palace revolutions. There have been directorial comings and goings in recent years at Aston Villa, Birmingham, Brighton, Crystal Palace, Manchester City, Portsmouth, Walsall, and on the lower levels as well. But these mean very little either to the public or to players, since the politics of football is out of the reach of the player or the normal type of club supporter.

*As things are players and supporters have virtually no say in what goes on. It is worth noting that one of the recommendations of the Chester Report was that the players (as well as managers and referees should be represented on the Council of the FA [see p. 86: this was no new idea]. But for that, as for much else, we wait with moderate patience. Supporters often suffer shabby treatment. A Supporters' Club more often than not is kept at arm's length by the board of a club, and yet this is the kind of association which really does have the interests of the game at heart. The man on the terrace certainly has more than a loud voice to contribute, and he should be taken into partnership. After all, so far as schools are concerned not only parents but also pupils now take their part in administration through management bodies.*

The ambitions and operations of a not untypical football club director make the right material for a John Braine novel. The object of the exercise – even if love of the game is written into any public utterance – is power. Now power by itself is neither good nor bad, just neutral. But power, alas, seems most often to be brought to bear in the wrong places and for the wrong reasons!

At the end of the road is the 'crock of gold' – the World Cup. For every little club the glitter of the World Cup is reflected in some other trophy.

Success at any level is important for a variety of reasons. Broadly these divide into two kinds. National success in football pays dividends in the currency of international prestige. In some countries this is emphasized more than in others. Elsewhere success in football gives a great fillip to commerce – and the entrepreneurs can make big hauls. The cries of misery that were heard when England failed to qualify for the World Cup of 1974 came largely from the multitude of commercial bodies which had their eager eyes on shares in a possible half a million pounds. Amid all this dismalling it was hard to hear any appreciation of the Scottish team which had succeeded in qualifying!

Increasingly a sportsman finds himself serving a whole

Above: Mike Kelly (Birmingham City) coaching schoolboys at Wall Heath, 1971

Below: Coaching course at West Midlands College of Education: F.A. coach, Keith Wright (kneeling) and John Bramley (with ball), with trainee coaches from U.S.A., Uganda and South America, and local youngsters

Far left: Determination in the Southampton defence, 1972
Left: Conversation piece; Roger Kirkpatrick and Terry Yorath (Leeds United) 1974
Bottom left: Avoiding contact; Derek Dougan leaps over Colin Boulton (Derby County) 1972
Below: Derek Dougan dealing with Emlyn Hughes (Liverpool) 1973
Bottom: A confident appeal; Wolves v Birmingham City 1972

Below left: Leaders of men: Charlie Roberts and his Manchester colleagues who gave a new meaning to 'United'

Below right: Northern Ireland players (1972) in London hotel before an 'away' game: l. to r. – Alan Hunter (Ipswich), Derek Dougan, Liam O'Kane (Nottingham Forest), Dave Clements (Everton), Willie Irvine (formerly Burnley and Brighton)

Bottom: Waiting for the match to begin; at the San Siro Stadium of Inter Milan

variety of masters. Some of them are in the background, unseen, but nonetheless powerful – and – because they are both invisible and powerful – sinister.

Exploitation is now wrapped up in the vogue word sponsorship. Once upon a time this was a noble word, a sponsor being one who 'promised solemnly for another'. In its crudest modern form sponsorship is to be seen in the cornering of practically all the tennis talent in the world by one oil millionaire. Cricket appears to have been saved by sponsorship – but sometimes by undertakings whose anxiety to have their products advertised, increased by restrictions on the advertising on the media of health-hazard products – is at least as great as their collective desire to redeem cricket.

The impossibility of veiling large lettering on the surrounds of football pitches from TV cameras has led to commercial interests renting space for advertising purposes in ever growing numbers. No doubt all this is for the good of the game. But it is difficult to restrain a certain cynicism.

There is a fair chance that the attitude of the advertising agencies, taking a cue from Madison Avenue, is: this is nothing to do with any players who may be involved. It might be pointed out, as a veiled threat, that this is the way for business to survive in the modern world. But its survival may very well be to the detriment of individual values and options.

A footballer is contractually bound to a football club; but he may find himself unwittingly obliged by the actions of that club to serve the interests of some other body. Let us take the position of a player who is by conscience a total abstainer from alcohol. What does he do if he is compelled to make himself a living signboard for a brewer, a distiller, or a wine producer? The chance of this happening may seem remote. But it is far from remote. The tobacco colossus, John Player & Son, spends vast sums annually on motor-racing. It maintains its own formula one team. This has been led by Emerson Fittipaldi – a non-smoker. Now let us look at the European football scene, starting with West Germany:

When the Hamburg Football Club jog out into the stadium this year [1973–4], they will be flaunting new football shirts, with the word 'Campari' written in blue letters on them. For last week, the club became the first Division One team to lease out its players' manly chests, in return for a juicy cheque from the Italian aperitif firm.

The first German club to accept such sponsorship was Brunswick, who inscribed the name of Jaegermeister, the Schnapps firm, on the players' shirts:

Just how much Hamburg got from Campari, when its team representative signed up on Wednesday remains a mystery. But Brunswick's five-year contract with Jaegermeister was worth £83 000 . . . 'We fail to see why footballers should not advertise in this way when many other sports do already,' says the West German Football Association. 'The real reason for dropping the advertising ban is the state of many clubs' finances.'

In Belgium a number of clubs are sponsored and players run out, therefore, with the names of travel agencies and car ferries emblazoned on their shirts. Are the players ever asked if this is the way they want it?

Not long ago the subject of League and F A Cup football being played on Sundays was a lively issue. To be truthful no one would have it produced as an issue except that the energy crisis made it one, and matches were only played on Sundays. Gates were up and it was concluded that because this was the case then Sunday football must be a good thing. No other consideration came under scrutiny. Certainly not the possibility that players might have their own views on the subject. One player, however, did strike a blow for freedom by refusing to take part in the exercise, and some clubs expressed their reservations on sabbatarian grounds. Apart from the matter of conscience there is the fact that players like to enjoy what is left of their weekend after Saturday matches. Some may very well be all in favour of Sunday football. But they should be consulted first and not last.

It will be seen that there are many ethical questions contained in a player's relationship with his employers, and with the public, which are either totally disregarded or simply ignored. A player is not someone's property to be disposed of according to expediency.

In 1970–1 sponsorship was introduced into English football

for the first time. After its introduction Alan Hardaker wrote about its scope and its possibilities. Hardaker saw a bright future for sponsorship and no chance that it would go the continental way. At this point one may wonder. One may also wonder at Hardaker's brand of semantics. Referring to the 'endorsing' (another meaningless vogue word in the advertiser's lexicon) of brands of alcohol or eau-de-cologne he states, 'This is not sponsorship, it is merely advertising which does nothing whatever for the game.' But Jaegermeister's agreement with Brunswick appears to be worth £83 000 to the game. And what is wrong with eau-de-cologne?

We must be quite clear about this. The only reason a sponsor throws himself into sport is so that he or his product will show up even more clearly on the screen for the benefit of millions than on the ground for the benefit of thousands and, with luck, to figure prominently in the pictures on the back pages of the popular national newspapers.

When it was agreed that sponsorship should be introduced into English football it was hoped that money would come in where it was most wanted. One may look back and regard this at best as a rather naïve hope. The principles that are the foundation of the practices of sponsorship are quite simple: they are that, by laying out money more money returns to the source. Sponsorship is a word that nicely veils the reality. The Football League, however, did its best to present commercial sponsorship in the best light. These principles were laid down:

(1) The sponsor to get a fair return for his money.
(2) The League and the game to benefit to the fullest extent.
(3) The spectator to be provided with an exciting form of Competition.
(4) Standards of dignity and administrative competence in the Competition to be upheld.

So far as (1) and (2) above are concerned their fulfilment must always be wide open to debate. What, for example, is 'a fair return'? What is 'the fullest extent'? In the oldest and biggest form of sponsorship (although in this case it is not called that), the pools, it is accepted that while (1) above seems to be satisfied, (2) certainly is not.

*I myself have always felt that the amounts of money received back in the game from the pools has not been enough.*

There is no dearth of regular competitions outside of what the sponsors may offer. There is no reason to suppose that they are deficient in excitement. Indeed, the FA Cup never fails to produce a real fever heat of excitement. While the long march towards the League Championship is a unique progress, followed in every detail by millions. The League Cup is not without its glamour. And then there is Europe.

It was small wonder that professionals had their doubts about some extra competitions. The Texaco Cup does, however, promote a wider British interest and on this account is worthwhile in principle.

*I would like to say from experience that so far as English and Scottish clubs are concerned, this competition has often aroused greater interest and brought bigger gates than some matches against European clubs.*

Alan Hardaker wrote that companies could not hope to achieve their objectives simply by advertising their products by means of the game. He advised that they could only be successful by displaying 'a genuine interest in the game'. Here one must think of the firms which across many years have done a whole lot for football and other sports by investment in their own sports amenities for the benefit of their employees. This certainly has been a worthwhile investment and one which has had far-reaching, though not generally appreciated consequences.

It all depends what the aims are. Here Hardaker warns us that 'the game's birthright must never be sold cheaply to a sponsor just for the sake of financial gain'. The most important part of his article runs on from this in unhappy sequence:

. . . Sponsorship is already bringing with it dangerous trends. The success of the three sponsored Competitions has attracted the attention of slick advertising agents, and the Football Association, the Football League, and the clubs themselves must be very cautious in dealing with approaches which are now being made. Efforts are being made to sell temporary advertising facilities on grounds where television cameras operate; efforts are being made to purchase from clubs the sole right to use their club badges; film clips from football matches are being used more and more in television advertising. These are just a few examples, and already one or two people have been tempted by what appears to be a good deal, from their point of view, but which could damage the whole idea of useful sponsorship by cheapening the image of the game.

That blend of piety and wishful thinking sounded distinctly out of tune with reality when it was issued. The nearer reality is set out in starker terms by Neil Wilson in the *Express and Star* on 12 January 1974. In a biting piece entitled 'The brand name of the game' Wilson refers to 'Big Brother Industry', pumping some £8 million of its advertising budget into sport. Soccer appeared to be the last to resist the kill. (As a matter of fact rugby football seems to be the last, for this – of all sports avowedly the least pecuniary and certainly not the most impecunious – has finally capitulated to the blandishments of the Smart Alecs of commerce.) Recently the FA invited commercial tenders. 'Even the FA Cup . . . could soon be sponsored if the price was right, say about £1 million.'

The Isthmian League has collected £40 000 for agreeing to add Rothmans to its title. Peterborough United are leasing advertising rights to a chain store company on the ground in return for £5000. Colchester United have drawn small sums from local firms anxious to imitate the big boys and get in on the sponsorship racket.

The basic cynicism inherent in the philosophy of contemporary sponsoring is wrapped up in the comments of the operators. Quoting from Wilson:

Gordon Ross, organizer of the 10-year-old Gillette Cup, told a sponsorship conference at London's Hilton Hotel this year that there was not a shred of evidence that it had sold 'one single razor blade'.

Watneys justified their soccer cup because of their market, the beer drinker. 'What do ordinary people like?,' asked their then promotions manager Stan Denton. 'Sex, football, beer. All right so we've got two out of the three.'

In February 1974 Watneys announced the end of the Watney Cup competition. With what they had achieved they claimed to be satisfied, but whether this back-out was of consequence to football was not mentioned. Presumably the promotions department, divorced from football, will pair their product with the other commodity detailed by Mr Denton, so that they will still claim to have 'two out of the three'.

Hardaker wrote of the danger of 'cheapening the image of the game'. What constitutes such 'cheapening' is a matter of opinion and taste. What is not is the affront on the dignity and the independence of the sportsman. 'He who pays the piper', writes Neil Wilson, 'largely calls the tune.' 'How much control can sport retain when it lives from hand to mouth off commercial charity?'

It is worth turning aside at this point to feel the full force of this statement. The Aintree racecourse lately passed from the Topham family to the Walton Group who are therefore responsible for the Grand National – that is, if there is a Grand National. The question is what happens if the BBC take the line which, by the terms of its existence, it is obliged to take that advertising 'must not be intrusive':

British Petroleum, who have just given up sponsoring the National, suffered from the BBC's inflexible ruling. Their executives studied film taken of 20 Grand Nationals when they took up their sponsorship and in every year they noticed the same hut appearing on film. So they had a large BP painted on the roof of the hut. It has not appeared on television since.

In the article in *The Guardian*, of 18 January 1974, in which this appeared, Mr Bill Davies, Chairman of the Walton Group, expressed his views in this charming manner:

What the BBC must realize is that they are not dealing with Tophams now. I think they are frightened to meet us now, because I have engaged the services of a top American who is an expert in the negotiation of TV contracts. But they'll have to meet me sooner or later and we'll get what we want eventually.

In the year 1972-3 ten English League clubs made profits. The other eighty-two lie waiting for the sponsor's kiss of life. This is the beginning of the process of exploitation. But it is not clubs which are exploited. It is people, in the final issue, players, whose rights and welfare are deemed secondary consideration.

*Thinking about the welfare of the player, with hindsight I can see how in the early part of my career I was manipulated, used, abused, and talked into hare-brained schemes. I can see all this happening this very day to inexperienced young men. It was with great sadness that I read of the tragic case of a once very famous footballer. He was 'taken up' by a certain company and*

launched on his new career (as salesman) with a champagne reception. He was photographed with his new company car surrounded by scantily clad 'dolly birds'.

*This world soon collapsed and difficulties not of his own making brought this footballer into the police court. His defence counsel said:*

He had been unemployed for several months. Then he saw the silver lining which one always hopes will appear. But it was really [his] good name and contacts the company wanted for their own ends. They used a name, of worldwide fame and internationally known, for the furtherance of the ends of the company. At some stage they were in serious financial difficulty ... This man was entitled to expect that his wages should be paid, but they were not ...

*I would advise any player, past or present, however much he may be flattered, to consider his own position before that of any supposed benefactor.*

The moral mess into which 'sponsorship' has led us is illustrated by the recent conflict between the Football League and the TV authorities. It was reported in the Press that the latter had offered £3·5 million for covering matches for a three-year period. Then a member of the League Management Committee, Lord Westwood, chairman of Newcastle United, pointed out in a statement that rather more than one third of this sum was to be obtained by the clubs out of ground advertising rentals. The Fulham chairman, Tommy Trinder, pointed out in a statement of his own that this must be a great deal less than satisfactory, because of the terms of the BBC Charter which bans advertising. 'The Government,' he added, 'has the final say with the BBC. So what happens, for instance, if they decide that the BBC must adhere strictly to its charter and we have to black out advertising spaces round the grounds.'

What is now called sponsorship used to be called patronage. A patron, however, was a person and not an anonymous company, and whoever was being patronized knew with whom he was dealing. There are some nice stories of the help which sportsmen sometimes obtained from the rich and influential in the famous books written about cricket long ago. The first of all great cricketers, John Nyren, for instance, writes with affection of a Duke of Dorset who helped all and sundry towards a career in cricket. The aristocratic founders of the FA were of this breed too. Their successors are still with us. But they are no more the real patrons of the game. Before the exponents of sponsorship they are, it seems, powerless.

A long time ago Samuel Johnson the great writer (who used to visit Wolverhampton) summed up the kind of sponsors he knew. A patron, he wrote, was 'one who looks with unconcern on a man struggling for life in the water and, when he has reached ground, encumbers him with help'.

The kind of relationship that exists between the footballer in an English club and the community of which he is a part gives another dimension to sponsorship. For the footballer himself while being used to promote other people's interests also has the chance as an individual of drawing attention to worthwhile causes.

*A lot of players don't realize just how powerful their position is in a local community. It is strange to reflect on this now, but I was once talking to George Best about his influence and the power he had to wield over a whole generation. It may seem incredible, but he was alarmed at all this. You are now able to see what has happened to him. And what has happened to him can happen to countless other members of the profession, if not to the same catastrophic extent.*

*There are demands from practically every walk of life. I don't think anyone else has such demands made on their private life. Most other people can escape into the privacy of their own home. Not a footballer who is 'in the news'. You are inundated with people coming to the door, with others telephoning, still others writing to try to get your ex-directory telephone number.*

*The Football club is a kind of generator, throwing out currents of human relationships in many directions. So one is forever going out to present cheques, to kick off at charity matches, to make draws, open fêtes, and so on. We are creatures of mood − like anyone else − and results of matches have a great bearing on mood. When one is having a bad spell there is a temptation to become a recluse. When one is doing well one faces the public with some confidence. I read enough newspapers to give me a fair idea of how I am doing in the public view. But whatever is printed there are obligations which come out of the popularity which the public has conferred on one. How fickle popularity can be is only too obvious. The other day a club programme carried a cover picture of the 'Player of the Week'. But he had been packed up and sold some days earlier!*

*The responsibilities of football rest on the players' shoulders. How often are chairmen and directors called out to open a centre for homeless or delinquent boys? Who is it who goes into the children's wards at the local hospital to cheer up the patients? The footballer gets landed with these tasks. In the one case it is hoped that 'good, clean-living, athletes' will in some way or other stimulate worthwhile ideas, in the other that they will be able to hasten the process of recovery. There is an element of folk-hero and magician about this. But however that may be, the calls on the young footballer's privacy are considerable.*

*I do believe that club directors, managers, and coaches, who have the right kind of experience, should help to educate players in the matter of public relations. A player is an asset to a community in more ways than one. I am sure that there would be handsome dividends in goodwill were young players shown how they could engage themselves in community affairs.*

*The future of our hopes in football − as in national life − depends quite simply on solvency. Within the game the available funds are insufficient when one thinks of the game in every aspect, and they are wrongly distributed. I remember talking to one director who had many years of experience and was on the board of one of our best known clubs. The theme of the conversation was the changes in the running of clubs that had taken place over the years. He said how he never thought he would see the day when a club had to rely on a social club, and a development association − whose main function is to sell bingo tickets although it tries to raise money in other ways, in order to make ends meet. But in the dog-eat-dog world of present-day football this is the*

K

*way it goes, and the way it must go unless other sources can be found to supply adequate funds. In the meantime clubs will go on appointing P.R.O.s and commercial managers whose job is to develop the financial side of the clubs.*

*As we have said, the few big clubs prosper, and they have everything in their favour. The British people are becoming very particular about where they go to see football and what they choose to do when they do go. So all ways they are demanding more of football on the spectator side. The media help to keep the momentum going in this direction. They concentrate coverage on the big boys. How many times is a Fourth Division match made Match of the Day? How much is there about lower division sides in the newspapers? The only time they come in for treatment is when they do a giant-killing act in the FA Cup. I know about that because it happened to me at Peterborough.*

*All through the game there is a lot of voluntary effort being made to keep the game alive at grass roots level. If all the people who make the effort to help football voluntarily were to withdraw their labour there would be absolute chaos. Football truly is a national matter, certainly as much as racing. Here we find discrimination. The British Government is Scrooge-like in its attitude to football relatively, generous about racing. The FA and League should be getting the best legal brains on to the job, to see what they would have to do to obtain the maximum grants from local and national authorities. At the beginning of this book the ideas of one visionary within the game foresaw the time when there would be government help. At present we have not got a visionary of this sort. What needs to be done is to see top class football not isolated but part of the whole soccer scene. One could wish for a start that the levy that is paid to clubs out of what the pools contribute (which is too little anyway) could be altered in the way it is paid out, so that the smaller clubs could benefit more.*

The necessity for something to be done is recognized by many influential people in public life. There are, however, too many who hope that the problem will simply go away. Dr Roger Bannister is not among these people. He states that sport and recreation should be regarded as an essential ingredient in life, and that in recognition of this the Government should make available much more in the way of funds.

Football has placed the authorities in a dilemma of their own making. As a result of Lord Wheatley's Report (see p. 31), a Bill was introduced into Parliament to compel those responsible for the maintenance of sports grounds (holding 10 000 or more spectators) to bring the safety of those grounds up to a required level. But it is uncertain exactly what can be quickly accomplished.

The FA and the Football League made it clear that in their view the Government should help to make such ground betterment as was required possible. Despite these and other pleas there has been no sign that there will be any assistance in the near future. However, there are those who look forward to a new relationship between football and the community to which it belongs.

In November 1973 John Morgan of the *Daily Express* wrote:

Soccer, half a dozen clubs aside, is a poverty stricken sport still clinging to a life-style that pertained half a century ago, yet we still have the same excessive numbers of stadiums, unused except for one day a week.

They should be replaced by municipally owned sports centres, of use to all the community, and rented by those clubs who can still make soccer a viable proposition.

A month later the Sports Council expressed the same opinion in another form:

... wherever possible professional football grounds should be developed to provide recreational facilities for the community.

The club would become a focus of sports activity every day of the week, and by this means could establish itself on a sounder financial basis, at the same time fulfilling a public service in which the local authority would almost certainly be interested.

English football clubs belong to the towns and cities whose names they carry. By their activities they make those towns and cities better known, and their citizens benefit in many and different ways. A famous team is a great aid to industry and business. A famous team is also a national asset. In this way football sponsors whole communities, and does so on the cheap.

*A football club is too important to be left to the mercies of the 'gnomes of Zürich' and their disciples.*

# 13. The Media

*'What is truth?'*

*The first thing a footballer does when he picks up a newspaper is to turn to the back page. This is what I have been doing all my life. Though in recent years I have run over the front pages – especially during the last couple of years when the lives and livings of everyone have seemed to be in jeopardy.*

*Most people connected with football normally start at the back of the paper and work to the front; some, of course, never reach the front. Eye-catching headlines hit the player straight away, especially when these have anything to do with the transfer market. Who knows when he is unexpectedly going to discover rumours about his own future in this way? The auctions that take place in the headlines may or may not have basis in fact, but they certainly destroy many confidences and much trust. It is the height of indecency when after one club has claimed to have set up a new record in transfer fees another, irked, rushes in to say that this claim is not true, and that its own figures in respect of such and such a player still stand at the top of the market prices.*

*The headline information about transfers is always mixed up with personality analysis. The player who is, or is to be, the subject of transfer rumours is 'discontented', 'fed up', 'unhappy', 'rebellious' . . . The awful thing is that, people look at this and think it must be true because the newspaper says what it says. Very often a close look shows that a newspaper headline says nothing at all. But how many of us do in fact look twice – unless it is about ourselves?*

*Does it matter what is said about people – other people, that is? One hears that people in the public eye should learn to live with criticism. Fair enough, but what we are worried about is not criticism but gossip. I suppose that George Best had his career ruined by headlines that had very little to do with what he is really like. The Welsh rugby international, Barry John, wrote how he had to give up his game altogether, because of the way in which the news media managed to make his private and personal life practically intolerable.*

*Naturally, any player wants to read the best about himself as a per-*

*former. If there is anything adverse in the way of comment and opinion it is passed over. If I go back in my career I remember the times when I would not read the papers after I had had a bad match. This was because the reporter would say something like, 'Dougan has stinker', or, '. . . he was never in the game . . .' Most times the reporter in question never said why. On a number of occasions I have asked a reporter who has written in this way why he thought I had played badly. Unfortunately it never seemed that he could offer any convincing analysis of my play.*

*So far as a player is concerned, he invariably has been trying to master his profession from very early days. As I look back I now realize that my profession really began when I was nine . . . So we may say that a player who has been through years of preparation 'knows in his bones'. This does not mean that he will necessarily be able always to explain what he is doing, or why he is doing it, but it does mean that he will know his craft in a way an outsider can't possibly know it. Benjamin Disraeli once said that critics were 'the men who have failed in literature and art'. In football most critics have not even got to the point of beginning to fail!*

*I do believe that this is the real bone of contention with players. They think that the average reporter who writes about football does not know his arse from his elbow!*

*I don't suppose the person who puts pen to paper about football sees it as his job to give critical technical advice. The general attitude is, he – or she – is only there to see a game and to report the facts of the crucial ninety minutes, or the facts that occur in the aftermath of a game full of incident. This faces us with other difficulties. There are facts, and there are what people think are facts. The famous winning goal in the World Cup Final between England and West Germany in 1966 was a goal because the referee said it was. That is a fact. It has always been argued by some that it was also a fact that Hurst's shot, after hitting the underside of the cross-bar, did not cross the line. Others, of course, said it did. Reporters divided in opinion according to their loyalties, and what were printed as facts were not so much that as opinions. This kind of thing goes on week after week, if not day after day. One is bound to think that the suggestion that a reporter is 'giving the facts' needs to be taken with a grain of salt.*

*One thing that we have to recognize, however, is that the Press have their difficulties. Not all players appreciate this nor, I suppose, most of the public. At too many grounds there is limited space for reporters. Sometimes there is not even a good view (not only at Stamford Bridge when the ground is in process of reconstruction)! Often the amenities are awful – think of the weather conditions facing reporters, not to mention photographers. The telephone line is frequently bad and – to crown all – at the other end there is a copy-taker who is totally uninterested. What is more is that for the vast majority of rank and file reporters their job has to be done in a hurry, in the knowledge that an edition has to be got out in next to no time.*

*The Press man could not do my job, and I could not do his. This means that there is a gap and it is a very difficult one to fill.*

*When one says 'the Press man' it sounds as though there is only one. There are almost as many reporters as there are footballers, for there is not the smallest local weekly that is without its football specialist. We have to be careful to distinguish between the best and the worst. When we think along these lines we become aware of the number of good writers who write about football. There are many more than there used to be, for this is in response to public demand. Because there are more, and because more people take in football at home through* TV *there are more literary minded writers in the field. Some of them give added colour and a sense of style. But the fact still remains that technical know-how and the ability to give a competent analysis of actual performance is limited. A lot of interest in the game is stimulated by speculation and there is even a kind of mysticism that surrounds it.*

*I must apologize if up to this point I have used the term 'Press man', although I did throw out a hint a line or two ago! We now have at least one 'Press woman' who has an enquiring mind, a fund of genuine enthusiasm, and a lively pen. Julie Welch of* The Observer *might like to give me some credit for her being where and what she is. It is always pleasant to find one's prophecies coming true – to be fair, to find one prophecy that has come true. In* Attack, *1969, I wrote:*

*Football is no longer the poor man's sport. It is everyone's sport. There was a time when a woman going to a football match was likely to be ridiculed, unless accompanied by her husband or boyfriend, in which case she was just tagging along to please him. Now it is not unusual to see women as unaccompanied spectators. Some may have a crush on a particular player, but they are outnumbered by those taking a serious interest in the game for its own sake. The day may even come when women sports writers take their place in the Press box.*

At the centre of things there is always tension. If tension within football seems to have increased it is because of increased tension outside. When I had been to America for the first time in 1967, after nine weeks I was glad to be back. It was so peaceful in England. Two years later I went to America again. This time when I came back I felt we were catching up rather fast. Tension in our society has quickened faster in the past decade than in the previous half century. To be fair, however, what with two world wars and mass unemployment the pace has only quickened on account of what went before. In football this is shown in perspective in Chapters 4 and 5.

Nowadays, however, news travels faster and there is more of it. Rather more news is needed. It is only a little time ago since Birmingham City played Newcastle United six times in as many weeks. They met twice in the Texaco Cup, on 22 October and 5 December (or rather three times because one game had to be abandoned on account of bad light). In connection with this it should be remembered that the Football League did not help matters by refusing a request to bring the game forward half an hour.

After a draw at St Andrew's in the League Cup on 30 October the teams met again in a replay at St James's Park on 7 November. Then, to crown all that, by pure coincidence there was a League match on 8 December at St Andrew's – just three days after the third Texaco Cup meeting. During the 5 December match Tony Want, of Birmingham, had his leg broken in the opening minutes in a collision with Jim Smith. This was unfortunate in itself. What was much more unfortunate was the fact that all sorts of talk was flying around outside the game at this time about vendettas. Much of the media took the line that what this or that player had in mind was, 'I'll get him this time'. In the words of Tom Clarke, of the Evening Standard, the way it was put in some columns was 'an invitation to a massacre if ever there was one'. I think that in these matches between Birmingham and Newcastle there were faults in the clubs and with the League, but the idea that the two teams were hell bent on crippling one another was sheer fantasy, although it would not be surprising if there were not some added tensions among the players on account of the Jim Smith–Tony Want incident.

In a recent Arsenal–Villa cup-tie there was what they call an 'incident' when Villa's Sammy Morgan ran into the Arsenal goalkeeper, Bob Wilson. He was sent off. The match ended in a draw. But before the replay the Press particularly built up the 'incident' as though it were *but one battle in a campaign, and before the teams had left the dressing rooms at Highbury after the first encounter the headlines proclaimed how Morgan was waiting for Wilson at Villa Park. This supposed personal rivalry (that never was) was so much written about that when Wilson appeared at Villa Park he was booed by some of the Villa partisans, and so was the referee, while Morgan was counter-cheered. In the event the game was a fine example of skilful football in dreadful weather conditions and equally a fine example of sportsmanship.*

*It is fair to say that when two teams are playing each other several times in a short space of time, it is only human nature for thoughts of possible retaliation to occur. Thoughts of this kind do not only affect my profession.*

*In contrast to the Newcastle–Birmingham encounters I would like to draw attention to the three matches we at Wolves played against Norwich City in the space of seven days in January 1974; twice in the League Cup Semi-final and once in the League. Talking of tension, this was then the situation. Norwich were hoping for a second appearance in twelve months, at Wembley, in the League Cup. They were literally fighting for First Division survival. Wolves, for their part, were fighting against a semi-final inferiority complex. In the previous season they had been, perhaps unluckily, knocked out of League and FA Cups, at semi-final stage, by Spurs and Leeds. Also at the time of these encounters between us and Norwich there were not many points separating the two teams in the League.*

*And what happened? The spirit and attitude of the two teams – if I may say so – was beyond praise. I went on record as saying that the semi-final of the League Cup against Norwich was the most difficult hurdle for me of the three semi-finals. But these games were played without incident. If people say – as they do – that sportsmanship is dead, then I would say they should have witnessed these three games. We did not, however, notice any complimentary banner headlines!*

*Eric Todd wrote about media exaggeration as one of the ills of the game in* The Guardian *just before Christmas 1973:*

Finally, managers, referees, and directors may well ask if some incidents on and off the field of play are not exaggerated or distorted by the media for the benefit of bloodthirsty readers and watchers. Ten years ago Dick Parker, a long-serving director and sometime chairman of Huddersfield Town, said: 'Are match commentators fair?

I think not. Newspapers magnify sidelines and insignificant incidents into dramatic stories and headlines. More coverage of the actual play is, I am sure, the desire of every football boardroom in the country.' Amen to that . . .

*I believe Todd has something there!*

*The Press will come back on this. On the bottom level the junior reporter will say he is doing what he is told. The senior reporter will have the benefit of the advice of the publicity boys on a paper. Sales are what count, and the utmost effort must be made to increase sales. Otherwise, it is argued, the paper will cease to exist. At the top level there is a strong feeling that the public must have what it wants. But what does it want? And who is it that makes it want what it is supposed to want? Somewhere at the bottom of this pile is the footballer – or any other sportsman in the public eye – and he may be forgiven if sometimes he feels more than a little cynical.*

The average footballer may sometimes seem to be a creature of whim but, if one looks from another angle, he may more often appear as the victim of whim. He himself doesn't probably put it this way, but he knows full well that writers have their favourites and also their 'unfavourites'. Of course this can rankle, and it is worth calling attention to one writer at least who understands. After the defeat by Poland in October 1973 the English Press became hysterical. One well-known journalist having forecast that England would win 4–0 was so downcast at his own failure after the match was over that all he could do was shout to all and sundry, 'What a bunch of bums!' Brian James, who was there to witness this change of mood caused by disappointment at being found fallible, and the behaviour of the Press men in general, wrote: 'One listened in vain for the sound of compassion for the men who deep below, in the dungeon of the England dressing room, sat alone with bitter thoughts!'

It was an American naval officer, Stephen Decatur, when fighting against the British more than 150 years ago who coined the phrase, '. . . our country, right or wrong'. One would have hoped that this had gone into limbo long ago. Alas, we know this is not the case! Pig-headed nationalism sometimes seems as strong as it ever was. This is why journalists scream when a football match is lost. They scream at the players, but most of all at the manager. Ramsey-baiting has been a journalistic pastime for years. It reached its peak of intensity a year ago. After analysing what Sir Alf was supposed to have done wrong in the eyes of the Press, Brian James had this to say:

His other major crime, of failing to take the Press into his confidence, of damaging some of their egos by not switching his long-range plans to take into account their wind-vane loyalties to different players, is not important; it clearly has no bearing on the tone of the witch hunt going on now. And his record of having won four matches and drawn another for each one that he lost is equally irrelevant at a moment like this.

But the spectators at the match, added James, did not see things this way. They saw a magnificent match, pulsating with endeavour, in which England's 'non-stop effort' and Polish 'courage and resilience' were generously praised. But it is the writers whose word lasts longest.

*It is a fact of football life that one is only aware of nationalism sometimes. For years I have played with Englishmen, Scotsmen, Welshmen, and Southern Irishmen in League football. Some of them are among my best friends. Yet every so often we find ourselves in opposing national sides and the media expect us to hate one another all at once!*

*Nationalism is an important part of football, and its place needs to be understood – not least by the journalists and commentators who make it such an issue. Sometimes this is in response to what is happening to the national fortunes in general. Too often, however, it is turned into a negative influence.*

*I suppose that I am less nationalistic than most people these days. Part of my inclinations in that direction departed from me on the boat from Belfast to Heysham in August 1957. Looking back – as one often does – this seems to be a contradiction, because when I signed for Portsmouth it crossed my mind that I might play for the Northern Ireland team one day. It's like when one does the pools every week – one expects sometime to win the jackpot.*

*When I was a boy of twelve I stood on the terraces at Windsor Park, Belfast, I never visualized the time when I would be in the company of*

*Messrs Blanchflower, McIlroy, Gregg, McParland, and so on. Yet it was less than a year before I wore the green jersey for the first team – during the World Cup of 1958.*

I had read that wearing the green jersey you became a different man. You were supposed 'to rise to the occasion'. These and many other clichés came from the Press in those days – as they still do. Nowadays I know for sure that I do not believe you become something special merely through the colour of your shirt. This myth is part of the media provocation. And, one may ask, how many of the media-men have ever worn the jersey of their country?

It is made clear beyond any shadow of doubt though that there is an intense rivalry between the different countries. This is most clear perhaps in Scotland, where defeat by England is something akin to sacrilege. It is always described as a 'bitter pill' to swallow (fortunately there is Scotch whisky to wash it down). And it is always a 'national disgrace' to be beaten. Confrontation may take place on the pitch and it may, and sometimes does, go on elsewhere. On occasion there has been more than an exchange of words in the Press box. I am convinced that the media have a heavy responsibility for building up a particular kind of tradition of national rivalry. This also becomes part of the spectacle as may be learned from any TV presentation of an international match.

Little Northern Ireland and Wales, of course, are only allowed by the media to go along to an International for the ride. We are certainly never expected to do well, and if we do (remember what Wales did to Poland at Ninian Park!) it is a great shock. A Welsh or Northern Irish victory is always 'totally unexpected', however good the players appearing in red or green jerseys. When Northern Ireland played England and I was in the team I knew something of what it was like when David took on the mighty Goliath. When we did come up with a shock result it was because we had George Best in the sling. And one then sometimes felt we were not playing fair by the Press to have such a match-winner in our ranks. There is a point at which a great player becomes as it were, de-nationalized, and described as 'world class'. But that, maybe, is only a form of supernationalism.

More than any other game perhaps the media can make or break an International. If it is the oldest of all Internationals – that between England and Scotland – which has been so long wrapped in a kind of mysticism – yards of print spread out to foretell a 'classic', or a 'battle', or both at the same time. Some of this feeling rubs off on to the players, *simply because they can't help themselves when they read what is printed about them.*

*There is the same kind of build-up for a Cup Final too. When so much is promised in Press and on* TV *there is every chance of an anti-climax. I am convinced that all the ballyhoo can have adverse effects on players. The case in point was the Leeds–Sunderland Final. Before that was played, so it seemed, Sunderland were not in with a chance. Afterwards, it was all up with Leeds. And after that judgment everyone knows what came next.*

*A journalist reports a game, but he has to edit what he might want to write. There is always the question of length, as well as other considerations, so that what could well go into thousands of words has to end up in a few hundred. Fifty years ago Hugh de Selincourt wrote 'The cricket match', a whole novel about one game. I am sure that one could find at least one football match which would provide material for one novel. But the reporter must put all ambitious ideas on one side. His job is to provide his copy in the form his chief and his public are used to.*

*It is forgotten that a reporter must do exactly what a* TV *editor must do – that is, cut out a lot of what takes place and concentrate on the highlights. One is aware of editing on* TV *more than in a newspaper simply because the picture on the screen is thought to be a truthful presentation of things. The camera can't lie. But can't it? That is why it can be a very bad witness. A skilled editor can so cut a film that a mediocre match can be shown as a much better one on the screen. The comparison can, of course, only be made by people who were at the particular match. When a whole match is screened this criticism does not apply, but even then the angle from which shots are taken can at least mislead.*

*In the past few years there has been a profusion of* TV *coverage of football. Maybe there will be less. However this may be, the blessings of this medium have been mixed for the others. Think of the reporter who has sent off his copy and then has to watch the match he thinks he described after his report is filed. It seems to him that nothing happened as he said it did.*

*Whatever may be said about the media in this connection it is certain that the centre of attention is the footballer himself. The media claim the right of freedom, and freedom of speech is something about which we must all be concerned. The right of the media to enjoy their freedom sometimes cuts down the freedom of other people.*

*The notion that a professional sportsman is entitled to his freedom is not always understood. It is the duty of the professional footballer it seems, to do, and not to think. Score thirty goals in a season, you are a hero. Score none, whatever the reasons, you are a villain. Within the limits of goals for and against, the striker at least, has his life in the media. Everything he does is related to his position on that map.*

The freedom of the footballer, then, is far from being absolute, although across the whole of this century there have been members of the profession whose ideals were centred on the theme of liberty. The old fighters for the rights of the professional footballer – like Meredith and Roberts of long ago – were, however, concerned with more than that. They saw the larger issues of which their complaints were but part, because they had educated themselves to understand the larger issues.

The penalties for not conforming to the standards imposed by superior powers in the more distant past were considerable. Meredith – the great Meredith, the 'Welsh wizard' of the Press – died if not in poverty then near enough to it to make no odds. Roberts – who may be seen in retrospect to have done more for the professional footballer than anyone else – played no more for England after he had opened his mouth on behalf of his colleagues.

It is a mistake to think that temporary affluence ('What do you footballers complain of – with no work – and £100 a week?') represents freedom. The better off among players – a small minority of the whole – are, of course, continual objects for appraisal and criticism in the media. Often one is aware that it is not they as performers who are under inspection but their image. And the comparison of the image a player presents is compared with the image he is supposed to represent.

In this connection it is instructive to note the process of downgrading that has taken place ever since the 1966 World Cup. (In retrospect, this event looks more and more a watershed.) We do not have to look into the files very far to discover that there are said to be no personalities in the game any more.

There was an article by David Sylvester in one of the colour supplements in which he drew attention to the 'new cult of personality . . . grown up around the figures who talk to the cameras about the game'. It may be that this new cult is in itself responsible for the idea (not one to which we subscribe ourselves) that there are no people with high individuality among the players. The 'pundits' (another loaded media term which goes along with 'experts' and 'authorities' to describe those whose qualifications may be questionable but whose confidence is unbounded) take players to pieces. Sometimes they exhibit them, on television or in the Press interview, taking care to show them as they should be. Gerhard Vinnai, in *Football Mania,* observes: 'monopoly capitalism has created information media in its own image, which replace information and argument by manipulation'. In another place in the same book the manner in which images are made in the interests of conformity to imposed cultural and commercial patterns is shown with startling clarity:

The interchangeability of stars and starlets from the worlds of film records, T V and sport is an indication that their appeal is by no means attributable simply to their own personalities. 'These stars . . . are themselves representatives of a higher authority; the authority of the prevailing social system' (quoted from H. Marcuse) . . . The idols of the manipulated masses only appear to have individual features; in reality they are products of their own advertising, symbols of social processes. The glorification of individual sportsmen only appears to serve the development of individuality; in reality it strengthens the constraints upon it.

In a world in which sponsorship plays such a large part, in which much of the media is involved with and dependent on the sponsors, it is small wonder that the situation is as it is. One is inclined to ask the media – for the faceless men who hold so much control – to consider their own responsibility for the supposed decline in the on-field presence of 'real individuals'. Are they not getting what they want by defining exactly what it is they want. A player is written about and often is written for.

'Readers' interest in football', writes Arthur Hopcraft in *The Football Man,* 'is insatiable, and it has been found to be intense at the level of chitchat. Newspaper circulations at their biggest are sustained by the unbroken flow of trivial detail as well as by occasional sensation.' Who wants the chitchat?

Who believes it? Who orders it? And who is it who asks the PFA 'to put their sorry house in order' under the caption 'Players must accept the responsibility?' Well that is from the Sports Editor of the *Evening Standard*.

Talk about dog eating dog! We came across this from Chris Lightbrown in *The Sunday Times*:

This season, the London Evening Standard, understandably irritated that most of its columnists from last season got into dispute with their clubs or asked for a transfer, dropped the lot and replaced them with a series of columnists whose main literary quality was that they were not likely to get into controversy or seek transfers.

The *Standard*'s columnists here referred to were in fact the ghosts of ghosts, the columns produced by them mutely eloquent of non-existence. 'There are', Lightbrown says, 'ground rules even in Toadstool Land. One is to steer clear of the real world at all times.' Toadstool Land is where the media put on wordage about football that is so pathetic that, in comparison, *Dixon of Dock Green*, or *Dr Who*, look like profoundly researched documentaries.

Does all of this matter at all? A good drama critic can be seen to be responsible for good drama. Bernard Shaw is one among numerous critics who have revolutionized the theatre in the twentieth century. There is still a vacancy for a football critic who can rise to these heights of knowledge and responsibility. When such a one appears the players will be the first to applaud his coming. For it is only when the truth is given with sympathetic impartiality that the professional footballer will feel able to exist as a person rather than as a shadow on a TV screen.

*The first and the last question of soccer in the media is what is wrong with it? The answer is simple. Everyone – including the media – wants to win. And everyone can't.*

# Some Recommendations

*by Derek Dougan*

1   *The Government of the Game*

It is beyond dispute that the three main bodies, FA, FL and PFA, should set aside their own vested interests and unite in the general interest, since there is so much at stake.

There are certain areas which belong to the authority of particular bodies, but on such issues as finance, domestic competitions and their planning (in which the present state of congestion makes for impossible situations), international relationships, real progress depends on a united front.

It is increasingly apparent that since football is a matter of national concern (on many different levels), and a strong social force, consultation with national and local government is a vital factor to be considered.

In recognizing the need for unity on the part of the football interests one also feels the necessity for a Department of Sport, headed by a man of stature with the title of Director, which can have lasting power to act.

Ten years ago there was talk in Parliament of a Sports Bill. It is incredible that nothing has in fact happened. The FA, the FL, and the PFA, all gave evidence to the Chester Committee and all that has happened to the conclusions of that Committee is that they have been left to stagnate – to the dismay of the PFA.

The necessity for more effective government concern was shown particularly at the time of the winter power crisis of 1974, when – in comparison with other forms of entertainment – football was shabbily treated.

Finance being at the heart of the matter, it is of paramount importance that a Football Levy Board should be established. This again must come from joint action by the controlling bodies of football. Who, one asks, will take the first step?

In the attempt to achieve unity the clubs must play their part. It is clear that some clubs are making progress in bringing their functions into line with modern thinking, but others are not. There is sometimes apparent a considerable difference between the way directors run their football clubs and their businesses outside the game.

Many clubs are faced with the problem of ground alterations, to conform to safety requirements. This affords opportunity to explore possibilities of productive collaboration. Clubs should obtain the best available advice as to ways in which they could benefit from central and local government support.

## 2    Club Structure and Management

In no case is there a 'divine right' for any one person, or group of persons, to have control. Whether it is a First or a Fourth Division club the aims and principles should be the same. The two major concerns of a club are, broadly speaking, finance and what happens on the field. To me what is most important is what goes on on the field. This is the yardstick by which everyone is judged, and success here begins to guarantee success on the commercial front.

The role of the director of a club has slightly altered over the last few years. It is recognized by some clubs that directors can be well employed if they have some specialist functions. For instance, one may have directors delegated to supervise finance, or administration, and one certainly might have people more directly concerned on the side of welfare. In many cases, of course, directors continue as they always did, and merely meet every so often without considering all the new demands that occur daily in connection with their club.

Management is best divided between specialists. There should be a Team Manager and a General Manager. In the old days a footballer more or less tumbled into management after his playing days were finished. It is now important that a player who aspires to management should begin to prepare himself properly for this role well before his playing career is over. In this connection it is worth mentioning that the PFA, in conjunction with the St Helens College of Technology, ran an important football management course in 1973, which covered every aspect of the subject. This shows how important it is for managers to acquire competence in the techniques of management by professional means rather than merely haphazardly.

## 3    Financing the Game

The main problem about finance is that people who are getting a lot out of football are not putting anything like enough in.

In the first place one is obliged to note how successive governments at Westminster have been quite indifferent to the needs of the game. Considering the contribution made by this 'cottage

L

industry' to the national life, it is scandalous that there is no recognition in terms of finance for my profession.

Do the pools promoters give enough to the game? I wonder what the attitude of the pools promoters would be should we organize our own football pools on a national scale. There is a reservoir of a million supporters, as well as all those countless millions who are TV followers of the game, who might approve such action, for the purpose of any such new pools project would be entirely to help the game. It is supposed that for a very long time to come a considerable degree of self-help will be required.

One outcome of a suitably ambitious scheme of this nature might be the building of a new super-stadium. With such a stadium, capable of holding a quarter of a million spectators, the eternal difficulty of FA Cup Final ticket allocations would be considerably eased if not completely solved.

It may be said that to start a major pools scheme would require much boldness. I do not believe that one should be timid.

If money were forthcoming all our grounds – whether in the First or the Fourth Division – could be developed so as to be much more widely used, and for all sports. In suggesting that some form of aid should be found from public funds one recognizes that there must be a *quid pro quo*. There are great possibilities here to be explored. On the local level one looks to the involvement of district and regional authorities in much the same way that they are concerned with theatres and other forms of entertainment and culture.

The long-term prospects of advertising revenue should be reasonable, but it is important that as much benefit should come to the game as to the advertisers.

The same applies to TV. Were we to have a sounder financial structure throughout the game we would be better able to negotiate profitably with the TV authorities.

The biggest difficulties centre on the existence of so many clubs that are near insolvent. These clubs were there long before the present crisis, but the bigger money involvements of the game underline their dilemma. At the same time, many of these clubs serve a more than useful purpose, and it is right that their needs should be properly taken into account.

## 4    Technical Matters

Should I remain in football and make it a full-time career I would want first of all to go to South America for at least a month, to study the very different techniques practised there. After that I would make a further pilgrimage, to Holland and to West Germany, for example. One must emphasize that one can never say that one has nothing further to learn. On the contrary, we have a great deal to learn from one another.

One would think that the FA and the FL might arrange visits by our most promising coaches and managers to other countries. There was a time when British coaches were thought to be the best in the world. The idea may still linger in some quarters, but it no longer really holds water. One might think that the concept of soccer as a world game might have taken a firmer hold than it has. But there is still a lot of parochialism about.

Throughout my career I have been continually asked why I had not bothered with the FA coaching schemes. I must confess that after seeing what kind of coaching has resulted over the last fifteen or so years I am not overkeen on the courses put on by the FA.

A few years ago I was talking to a colleague who told me how in one club to which he belonged eight members of the first team undertook coaching courses. Within two years they were all qualified coaches – but the club, unfortunately, was relegated. I believe there may be a moral here.

It must be said, however, that courses have taught many players how to set about coaching, and has helped in laying foundations for some managers.

There is no doubt that so far as training is concerned we have made much progress, so that there are probably no fitter players than the British anywhere in the world. But sometimes I think that we spend too much time on the physical aspects of training, especially at youth level.

This is an area where one would again like to see unity of approach, with the FA, the FL, and the PFA acting jointly. If we had our own centres the PFA could exercise a particularly beneficial influence.

Should we have professional referees? This is an issue that has many implications and has become prominent in recent years. Does it mean that referees should be full time? Does it mean that referees should get more money? Or does it mean that ex-professional footballers should become referees?

(1) The Referees' Association must be established so that it is a body quite independent of the FL. That is fundamental.

(2) The PFA could confer with such a body and discuss the most important issues.

(3) There should be opportunity for ex-players, with intimate knowledge of the game, to become professional referees within a

period of, say, two to three years. This would enable people of great experience to plough this back into the game.

## 5 The young Player

With the raising of the school leaving age the apprenticeship of boys to football takes on a new complexion. At the beginning it must be recognized that those who are interested are able to have adequate tuition in football both at school and during their holidays, provided that everyone works together.

When I was a boy it seemed that sport and education were incompatible. I know now that I was wrong, for the two not only can but must go together. I am constantly telling boys this. A few years ago I was asked if I would like my own boys to be professional footballers. My reply was that I would like them to go to university and get degrees. It is now possible to do both. A footballer who is adequately educated is, in the end, a better footballer.

My advice to today's players is that they should consult their own organization, the PFA, over their problems, whether these are educational, contractual, disciplinary, or even personal and domestic.

## 6 The Media

One should advise any young player never to reply to questions put to him by the media without giving the matter a proper amount of thought. Professional sportsmen are chased around by the media, and at times it seems that your life is not your own. The sportsman is told, 'It is your duty to say so-and-so . . .', or, 'It is your public duty to reply . . .' As I look back I would not like to relive the years between eighteen and twenty-five. This is the time when reputations are made or marred, and the young man can be badly hurt by the effects of publicity.

## 7 Contract

I would like to see implemented:
(1) Freedom of contract.
(2) A pension scheme for all members of the PFA.
(3) Opportunity for players to become professional referees.

A.D.D.

# Sources Consulted

Apart from local and national newspapers (significant references to which are attributed in the text), the more obvious popular football literature, and documents made available and acknowledged in the Introduction, the authors have made use of the following:

*Report of the Committee on Football* (the 'Chester Report'), Department of Education and Science, HMSO 1968.

*Report of the Inquiry into Ground Safety at Sports Grounds*, the Rt Hon. Lord Wheatley, for the Home Office, the Scottish Home and Health Department, HMSO 1972.

*Commission on Industrial Relations, Reports no. 37 (1972) and 40 (1973)*, HMSO.

*Code of Industrial Relations Practice*, Department of Employment, HMSO 1971.

*FA Year Book*, volumes from 1950–1: official publications of the FA.

*The Football Association Handbook, 1973–4*: official publication of the FA.

*The Football League Handbook, 1972–3*: official publication of the FL, issued from Lytham St Annes.

*League Football*: official journal of the FL.

*Association Football*, ed. A. H. Fabian and Geoffrey Green, 4 vols., London 1960.

*Football as Popular Culture*: an outline prepared for the Centre for Contemporary Cultural Studies of Birmingham University, C. R. Critcher, 1971.

*Football Mania*, Gerhard Vinnai, translated from the German, London 1973.

*Football Fitness*, Bill Watson, London 1973.

*Foul, the Alternative Football Paper*, monthly publication.

# Index